Spirit of the Dancing Warrior

Spirit of the Dancing Warrior

Asian Wisdom for Peak Performance in Athletics and Life

Jerry Lynch and Chungliang Al Huang

Amber Lotus Publishing
Portland, Oregon

Published by Amber Lotus Publishing
P.O. Box 11329, Portland, Oregon 97211
800.326.2375 • www.amberlotus.com

Amber Lotus Publishing first printing: 2010
10   9   8   7   6   5   4   3   2   1
Printed in Korea

Library of Congress Control Number: 200937534

Cover and book design: Leslie Gignilliat-Day
Cover and interior calligraphic art: Chungliang Al Huang
Editorial services: Meadowlark Publishing Services, www.larkonline.net

Amber Lotus first edition ISBN: 978-1-60237-364-8

Dedication

To anyone who decides to read this work: you are a Dancing Warrior Spirit but may fail to recognize it because it has been lying dormant within. The Tao would suggest that you simply notice this and then act accordingly.

Acknowledgments

Much gratitude, appreciation and heartfelt love to Lawson, Leslie, and Tim, the Dancing Warriors at Amber Lotus, for their extraordinary wisdom, sensitivity, vision, and integrity throughout the entire process of this joyful project. It truly has been an amazing dance.

Contents

Part IV: Transformation
From Sole to Soul

Epilogue: Completion
From Tao to How

Introduction: Connection
From God to the Games

There it was. Positioned squarely on the front page of the daily sports section, the Associated Press piece announced "God at the Games." Like clockwork, the arrival of the Olympic Games ushers in an abundance of enthusiasm and curiosity about something rarely discussed yet universally sensed: the intimate connection between sport and spirituality, between the outer sole of our athletic shoes and the soul within.

Seeking this connection between the two are athletes of all faiths: Christians, Muslims, Hindus, Jews, Buddhists, and others. A special, sacred relationship seems to help these devoted athletes gain a broader perspective on competition, achieve greater self-understanding, develop a deeper sense of the role of sports in the bigger game of life, and enter an environment for peak performance.

This relationship comes as no surprise to us, Jerry Lynch and Chungliang Al Huang. We don't need the Olympics to remind us of this special connection. We work with thousands of athletes, martial artists, dancers, performers, and fitness enthusiasts who demonstrate such "godlike qualities" as courage, compassion, fearlessness, and joy, and who seek ways to nourish their souls through physical activity. Martha Graham, the famous American choreographer, called her dancers "the Acrobats of God," marveling at their seemingly superhuman powers. Nijinsky, Nureyev, and Baryshnikov are other heavenly athlete-dancers who come to mind.

This body-spirit connection is certainly not a new concept. Many ancient holy books, such as the Torah, Koran, and Bible, teach that the care of the body is indeed the care of the soul.

Our combined experience as athletes, teachers, and authors of several books on the body-spirit connection tells us that there is worldwide interest in this intimate relationship, in something beyond scores, laps, miles, reps, and other external rewards the physical life offers. Legions seem to be in search of richer—and at the same time, more practical—spiritual experiences in life. Athletics and fitness can serve as vehicles to transport us to a more sacred space, perhaps to a closer relationship with God or Buddha, in every arena of life.

Spiritual Vitamins: Supplements for the Soul

When you open your heart to the special connection between the physical and the spiritual, whether in the gym, on the field, practicing Tai Chi, or riding your bike, you expand and improve your experience and performance—and your relationship with *all* physical activity. We have written *Spirit of the Dancing Warrior* to assist you on this path, filling it with information on practical spirituality and how to use it to achieve peak capacity in all your physical work and play. It will help you develop stronger, more meaningful relationships with your sports and fitness regimens—and with yourself—as you apply its lessons. It provides spiritual warrior training: concise, practical, sacred gems and soulful nuggets that nurture quiet meditation, motivation, empowering inspiration, wisdom, and excellence. These spiritual vitamins will boost the Warrior Spirit of your physical life, infusing it with extraordinary vibrancy, excitement, and joy. You will experience revitalization and transformation as you journey toward excellence, emerging with a stronger mental focus and a clearer frame of heart.

Our aim for this book is to help you reach these goals, not only by showing you what we have learned from our years of involvement with athletics, fitness, martial arts, and dance, but also by leaning heavily on the ancient wisdom of the *Tao* (pronounced "dow") and Zen Buddhism. Applying Eastern philosophy to such spiritual training offers a natural, practical, and simple approach encompassing daily meditation, inspiration, affirmation, and education—all of which lead to greater wisdom. You will become simultaneously more awakened and grounded prior to, during, and following your physical experience. As you navigate the challenging pathways between sports and spirituality, this book can serve as your companion. It can help you transition enjoyably from the mundane daily concerns and ordinary realities of life to the realm of extraordinary sports and exercise. You will feel more alive, focused, happy, and motivated. Here is a way, a Tao, of entering with the body, mind, heart, and soul of the warrior the worlds of athletics and fitness—and the fullness of your life. This is a journey from ordinary to extraordinary. As your performance improves and you obtain deeper spiritual wisdom in the process, your relationship with all physical activity will begin to change.

For many athletes and performers, the relationship between sports, movement, fitness, and life can often be confusing, filled with conflict and strife. This may reflect an existential gap between how they train and perform and their deeply held values and ideals, what we call soul: those warrior qualities—such as honesty, integrity, reliability, dependability, courage, patience, and perseverance—that really matter and make a difference. Many fail to realize the connection between physical activity and the important role these spiritual qualities play within their hearts. They truly want to demonstrate integrity, for example, yet are either unaware that they do or are not sure how to accomplish it.

Who wouldn't want to experience a soulful connection and relationship with something greater than themselves? You can begin to transform and strengthen your relationship with any physical activity in life by choosing the higher road, where the effort shifts from the exterior battlefields of time, score, or opponent to an interior terrain: overcoming fear, failure, and self-doubt. You win these battles with weapons of the heart, warrior virtues that will help connect you with your fearless, tenacious, and courageous self on the path to discovering your greatness.

You will learn the power of the gut (the Asian *hara* or *dantien*), focusing on the center, the original of all movement where the warrior's physical power resides. This is where profound transformation can occur as the physical becomes the conduit for spiritual growth and change. You will begin to live, play, and compete with heart and gut aligned, in the sacred space of greater meaning and value for all your emotional and physical needs and accomplishments. Your soulful efforts in this work are more powerful than any perceived obstacle. This is the true essence of what we call Spirit of the Dancing Warrior, the path of spiritual training to journey toward excellence.

The Format of this Book

We would like to call your attention to this book's basic structure. The main body of the book, beginning with Part I: Intention, comprises four distinct parts representing the four seasons. In Chinese culture, the full cycle of the seasons represents a complete experience, marking lasting change in habits and perceptions. And so, we ask you to give yourself the entire year to steadily transform your relationships in sports, fitness, and life.

The four parts of this book are further divided into fifty-two distinct warrior virtues—ideals, concepts, or traits—one for each week of the year. Within each you will find the virtue (Emptiness, for example) described, followed by a declaration and a reflection. The declaration is a strong, affirmative statement that will crystallize and reinforce the lesson to be learned and practiced each day of that week. The reflection offers you an opportunity to contemplate the virtue's wisdom by answering pointed, self-motivating questions about it that will help you apply and embody each one. Together, these elements serve to guide you in your sport, fitness regimen, and daily life. On the opening page for each virtue, for your aesthetic enjoyment, you will find Chungliang's beautiful calligraphic artwork depicting the essence of the particular concept being presented. These Chinese images will themselves create a strong impact on your body, mind, and spirit by capturing the Tao and Zen principles as visual, kinesthetic, and holistic symbols.

• • •

Before we go further, here at the outset of this spiritual training, there are a few things we need to mention so we don't give you the wrong impression.

We do not intend *Spirit of the Dancing Warrior* to be a scholarly work on Tao and Zen. Rather, our hope is that it provides you with a Tao—a way or a path—to help you on your journey from ordinary to extraordinary as you train, compete, and live in alignment with your heart.

We chose to write this book in the spirit of giving and sharing our love, passion, and experience; it is an attempt to give back. We hope you will take this sacred spiritual ball and, by applying its lessons and wisdom to your own life, run with it toward genuine winning. We want you to see and feel your physical efforts through an expanded lens and with an open heart as you revamp your beliefs and perceptions of what is possible on this warrior journey from sole to soul. This is what is referred to in Zen as the cycle of Buddhahood—and what we affectionately call "being in the 'hood."

Prologue: Creation

From Mindfulness to Warriorship

You are about to embark on a program of everyday spiritual training, a soulful path of wisdom, inspiration, and motivation for athletics, fitness, and life. It is truly a creative process, one of intention, preparation, integration, and transformation of all aspects of the self. As you travel on this journey, you will establish a new and exciting warrior relationship with yourself and with all your physical pursuits. You will create an inner environment of mindfulness where personal spirituality can be nurtured and nourished. You will practice emptying the mind and filling your heart with the virtues and traits of the warrior as you navigate the four sections of this book, the four seasons of change—from ordinary to extraordinary, from Buddha to Bob Marley, from thinking body to dancing mind, and from sole to soul.

Mindfulness

The Chinese symbols for mindfulness are *yi* and *nien*. With *yi* we have the "music from the heart" that gives us the immediate and dual sensory experience of hearing and feeling the vibration of the sound from within. With *nien* we experience the visual and auditory image of the sound of a bell ringing in the here and now, in our heart/mind center of consciousness, as we become fully awakened with all of our sensory perceptions. In its purest form, mindfulness leads to a state of relaxed consciousness, awareness of the implications of our actions, decisions, movements, and words. We pay attention to what is. For example, when mindful, we do not talk about our successes with one who is in pain or experiencing failure.

As a result of this focus, attending to the yi with the nien, you can experience profound joy and high levels of self-mastery. As Asian wisdom poignantly expresses it, the focused mind can pierce through stone.

According to ancient Taoist tradition, it is practically impossible to achieve excellence and extraordinary performance without daily solitude: a time of retreat, reflection, rejuvenation, and restoration of *chi*—the source of physical, emotional, and spiritual energy. Such peace and quiet can be attained in many ways. For example, in Chinese, the expression *shang shan* suggests ascending to the mountaintop in order to escape the chaos and pressures of daily life. The summit provides a sanctuary, a natural, sacred meditative space of peace, relaxation, and clarity of thought. Another Chinese concept, *gui shan* (literally meaning "returning to the mountaintop"), implies an effortless settling in to a comfort zone of being completely in the here and now. In philosophical and psychological terms, this summit or mountaintop is a place where you are always in perfect harmony, balance, and ease.

You may have noticed that animals instinctively know and use a method of stillness in nature. They all meditate. Observe the heron poised motionless on one leg, the monkey climbing to the uppermost branch, the snake basking in the warmth of the summer sun, or the cat lying on a pillow, eyes focused on a small object. Such stillness prepares the inner environment for a deep, peaceful *meditative* state in which clarity can be realized.

To help you achieve such solitude, we offer you our version of meditation, one that draws from slow, deep yoga breathing. It will clear and free the mind and create a state of in-the-moment mindfulness. We must tell you, though, that there is no path to mindfulness; mindfulness is itself the path. Such a path can easily contribute to extraordinary performance, as we have observed with thousands of world-class and professional athletes and masterful martial artists who use this technique. The breath we refer to is soft, yet strong. There is an Asian adage: "If you know the art of breathing, you have the strength, wisdom, and courage of ten tigers." The inner calm and stillness created through this special, foundational breathing technique becomes the basis for exploring your personal greatness, and it provides you the opportunity to look at yourself and become fully human on the path of the warrior.

Practicing meditation is not complicated. We are not asking that you become a Buddhist monk and sit *zazen* eight hours a day. Although this would have merit, you may find it difficult to add yet another obligation to the long list of to-dos in your very busy life. Realizing this, we have designed a simple, practical spiritual training method that requires a minimum of eight to ten minutes at a time, during which you read a virtue, trait, or concept, then meditate, visualize, affirm, and reflect upon what you've read. We believe that such short meditations are helpful and much better than not doing any at all. The key is consistency, however, and like any skill, meditation takes practice. In this way, it is not different from learning to hit a golf ball, shoot a foul shot, or roll a bowling ball. The more frequently you practice, the more proficient you get and the easier it becomes. If you want to go deeper, you may want to investigate and experience the practice of Tai Chi, which is often thought of as stillness in motion and is considered by many to be the ideal way to meditate for mindfulness.

We also recommend a variation of a form of meditation called *vipassana*. Ours is a slimmed-down version of this most popular form of Buddhist mindfulness. Its purpose is to help you to focus your attention and awareness in the moment, to be more mindful in the here and now, and to live your physical experience more fully with a greater sense of freedom, happiness, and well-being. Buddhists refer to this state of mindfulness as the "Buddha nature." In Chinese, it is referred to as *wu shi*. For the purposes of this book, we call it "Warrior Spirit," the way of the warrior within.

Now let's take an in-depth look at the concept of the warrior, its symbolic origin, and the practical application of the heart- and mind-set of true Warriorship.

Wu Shi: The Warrior Spirit

The first warrior was the hunter armed for battle with a spear, fighting animals for safety and gathering food for survival. As humans became more civilized, the warrior became the hero, a person with many godlike traits and virtues. According to ancient Taoist warriors, the power of honorable traits was greater than the power of arms. They desired to solve conflict peacefully and created a fine balance between conquest and surrender. Weapons were used only when all other options had been exhausted. Taoist warriors were realistic, acknowledging their need and asserting their right to self-defense. In their godly attempt to avoid war, they sought victory through political and diplomatic means before war began, often avoiding fighting altogether.

Eventually this ancient concept developed into the warrior-hero, a more evolved, cultivated person such as the samurai and Kung Fu master. In Chinese, the warrior is described by the two symbols *wu shi*. *Wu* shows the spear at rest, philosophically depicting the real true power of the Warrior Spirit, the warrior who does not need battle to be a hero. *Shi* represents the cultivated, learned, civilized person of limitless potential. When the two concepts combine as one, wu shi, or Warrior Spirit, is about being physically, spiritually, emotionally, and intellectually alive in accordance with nature. It is the approach to cultivating your potential for peak capacity and the highest possibilities through the use and application of rigorous spiritual training that we refer to as Warriorship.

Let's take a minute to become familiar with the intricate aspects of this concept.

Warriorship

It is said that in ancient Tibet several mystical, legendary kingdoms existed. One such mysterious place was Shambhala, located high in the Himalayas. Here was a culture of enlightened, heart-awakened warriors, valiant fighters of compassionate, courageous, and indomitable spirit. They were considered brave athletes of iron will who faced their fears and rose from the dark depths of frustration and self-doubt through humor, inspiration, and wisdom. These Zen warriors were armed with such intangible weapons of the heart as fearlessness, patience, integrity, courage, tenacity, and fortitude. They perceived all obstacles and mistakes as opportunities to learn, grow, and become more aware of the greatness that comes from within. According to the legend of Shambhala, only these brave warriors, those who were pure of heart, could experience this mystical territory, known to Westerners as Shangri-la. This stuff of warriors, these qualities of the heart, is part of what we know as Warriorship.

For practical purposes, we define *Warriorship* as a "heart mind-set" whereby you sacrifice for others, push past your breaking point, have no regrets, and work hard even when others are not looking. You accept responsibility, remain accountable, and strive to win, but you do not need to win to be successful. You accept opponents as partners and understand when soft is strong, when less is more—you think outside the box. As a warrior, you become comfortable with being uncomfortable; you are willing to suffer, sacrifice, and fail if that's what it takes; and you enjoy the journey and do the best you can in all arenas of life.

There are no prerequisites of age, size, or shape to become such a warrior. In our work we have encountered this warrior posture and attitude in eight-year-olds and eighty-year-olds. We know a seventeen-year-old runner who was not the most gifted or talented, yet who, by being fully marinated in these warrior mind- and heart-sets, managed to garner a second-place finish in his quest for the state cross-country championship, earning a college scholarship in the process. There is the story of a sixty-five-year-old man who, contrary to the advice of his peers, chose the path of the warrior and planted an apple orchard. They told him he would never live to see the trees bear fruit. When he turned ninety-two, his wife made him a pie with apples from those trees to celebrate his birthday. His warrior mentality helped him live with gusto and a deep sense of purpose. He realized his dream because of his heart-mind approach to life.

So, as you might imagine, Warriorship is a rigorous spiritual training that awakens all who take the journey to higher levels of personal performance. *Spirit of the Dancing Warrior* relies on this ancient tradition while providing a valuable modern application of such training for athletics, fitness, and present-day life. In the words of the Chinese sage Lao Tzu, "Keep the ancient, flow with the present." You need to know this: the Warriorship Way is a never-ending journey; mastering it simply means staying on track. Our book is meant to help you to do just that, to keep you on this path throughout the year by meditating on each concept as it relates to the Warrior Spirit and how it applies to increased levels of self-mastery.

Practical Four-Step Spiritual Warrior Training

Meditation

A warrior needs to gather energy (chi), calm the body, clear the mind, become free of fear, and have the courage to compete all out in athletics and in life. To help our clients accomplish these things, we teach them the practice of meditation, a state of inner quiet and peace. Taoists call this sacred space the still point, a place that raises awareness, creates effortless movement, increases confidence, and regulates emotional weather patterns.

Not many know that Tiger Woods, the epitome of focus and calm on the golf course, learned meditation at the age of six from his Buddhist mother. Our friend Phil Jackson, coach of the Los Angeles Lakers, has always encouraged his players to meditate prior to a game in order to connect more strongly to the team's mission and goals. And we want to help you find your still point with a combination of Zen meditation, yoga breathing, and imagery psychology.

The form of meditation we teach is simple and to the point. Sit under a tree, in a chair, on a bench, or anywhere you can be free of distractions, noise, or interference. Close your eyes to better concentrate and begin to focus on the natural movement of your breath. See and feel it as it makes its way through the nostrils and into your lungs. Follow the breath as it exits the body through the nostrils and evaporates into the air. Repeat this process for about four minutes each time. If your mind wanders away from the breath, simply say silently, "Wandering … come back," and notice the breath again.

The key to this meditation is to release the tendency to control the mind's wandering. You achieve success when you do not bring the mind back by force but instead let your focus return to the breath naturally, like a boomerang, effortlessly coming home. When it does, you experience *satori*, the perfect space of the here and now.

This meditation will quiet and clear your mind in preparation for the next phase, visualization. Because you have emptied the mind to a degree, there is much more room for the images and concepts on the page to enter your nervous system. This creates a positive effect on your body, mind, and spirit. It directly affects your performance, putting it in harmony with the lesson being learned.

If you decide to omit the meditation stage altogether as you work your way through the fifty-two concepts in this book, reading the passage and thinking about how it relates to you and your activity will still create profound results. But like a sponge, the mind works best when less saturated. When you meditate and empty the mind, you create greater awareness and inner calm, and the benefits are exponentially more powerful, joyful, and fun.

Visualization

By pacifying stress based on projection, true relaxation can be attained. What springs forth will be in accordance with your real needs.

I Ching 52

Once your mind has narrowed its focus to the simple act of breathing, you are now ready for visualization, the second part of the spiritual warrior training, in which you steep your nervous system in the wisdom and inspiration of the virtue, the sacred gem of the week.

Visualization is a natural skill that can be taught and learned. It is an active, intentional effort to choose appropriate images of success while in a meditative state in order to influence your body's response to circumstances. Visualization for enhanced performance is not new; sophisticated athletes, dancers, businesspeople, and others use it, refusing to leave the outcomes of their work to chance.

Visualization works because it cues the body to synchronize millions of neural and muscular activities. Through constant practice, the central nervous system will interpret the images the mind develops as if they were real. As a result, what you visualize can have a powerful impact on every cell in your body, activating the appropriate muscles for the activity desired. In addition to visualization's effect on muscles, research conclusively demonstrates that it can be used to change blood pressure, heart rate, body temperature, and other functions of the body. Physicians use the technique at major cancer and heart research facilities to help patients in the prevention and healing of serious disease.

Unlike others, who teach visualization as a process of seeing an image, we prefer to not just see but to feel the image as well. In other words, we ask you to fill yourself with the *feelings* of movement, joy, appreciation, sadness, excellent performance, or anything else the written passage of the week may suggest. For example, *feel* yourself being fearful and then feel yourself coming through it. Feel what it is like to yield, to have integrity, to be moderate, selfless, or trustful, or to demonstrate a beginner's mind. Use the text as a guide to keep you feeling the essence of that particular concept.

To illustrate the power of visualization, we would ask you to sense the difference between seeing a yellow lemon wedge on a plate and biting into and tasting the sour fruit and feeling your salivary glands respond to this experience.

As a further example, you can see yourself running, biking, swimming, or lifting weights, or you can feel the sensations you have when performing such tasks: the ground beneath your feet, the breeze in your hair, the smell of the trees, the speed of your pace. This feeling approach is much more meaningful, powerful, and long-lasting, creating a stronger body-mind-spirit connection and response. It makes the experience more real and is likelier to deeply affect behavior and performance. Remember, the central nervous system doesn't distinguish between real and imagined events; it responds to all images as if they were real. If, for example, you sense yourself running strong and relaxed, you will feel inner calm and confidence, and your performance will reflect that.

Visualization works because it is a dress rehearsal that familiarizes you with the real task that lies ahead. It is a learned skill you can improve by practicing consistently. When the time comes to move, you already have the sense that you've "been there, done that."

Declaration

After you read each passage and practice meditation and visualization, you are now ready to include the third part of the spiritual warrior training: the declaration or affirmation, a self-guiding touchstone or prayer that will summarize, reinforce, and validate the sacred contents of the preceding message. Unlike visualizations, which involve what you see and how you feel, these strong, positive statements influence what you say and how you think. Your thoughts strengthen or weaken you and determine the direction in which you go. To demonstrate this, you can say out loud: "I can do this; I am a strong, vibrant, talented, physically fit athlete." Notice how excited, hopeful, motivated, and confident you feel as you recite these upbeat, positive words. Now notice the difference when you say: "I can't do that. I am a weakling wimp."

Affirmations are spiritual gems that will keep you on the warrior path and provide guidance to get back on track if you fall off. We suggest that you write your favorites on index cards, one per card, and refer to them often throughout the day or week, as needed. When you declare these words to yourself on a regular basis, your behavior will begin to reflect what the words express. Essentially, when you act the way you want to be, you will be the way you act. In time, you become these words; the words *are* you and they have a positive and profound effect on all aspects of your life. Conclude your meditation and visualization ritual with these powerful statements and self-guiding phrases. Remember: what you say as an affirmation may not be true in this moment, but that doesn't matter. The words are simply self-direction, not self-deception.

Reflection

Finally, in the fourth part of your spiritual warrior training, we encourage you to take sufficient time to reflect upon and answer the questions that follow each declaration. Each one is a practical road map and will help guide you from the inside out on your journey from ordinary to extraordinary; it will help you seek proper, useful direction. You may think of reflection as a quest: words that act as a vehicle for change and help you move forward. The questions encourage you to continue the work that needs to be done in a practical, efficient way in order to expand upon what you have learned in the passage. If you take these inquiries to heart, sincerely answering them as they relate to your unique circumstance and taking the appropriate action, you may very well attain a new level on this warrior path.

All great discoveries, all worthwhile accomplishments in life originate with questions that guide and accelerate progress. This is why we have included these question guides. In Zen practice, the ultimate question, the *koan* offered by the master, is truly the unanswered question, meant to be answered for yourself, not by the master. When you get your answer, you achieve clarity and the question disappears.

Part I: Intention
From Ordinary to Extraordinary

We now enter the first stage of the journey of the Spirit of the Dancing Warrior: *intention*. In this part, your primary intention is to discover how to play, train, compete, work, and live in alignment with your heart. When you do so, you mitigate pressure, tension, fear, and frustration. The Buddha said it so eloquently: "Your work is to discover your greatness and with all your heart, give yourself to it." When you function from a heart-space, you enjoy the journey, exist in the moment, and focus on what can be controlled rather than fixating on the results and what you cannot control. You demonstrate integrity, affirm yourself and others, and seek the extraordinary in each day.

Spanning a period of over forty years, we have been associated with extraordinary performers of all ages in many disciplines, including athletics, business, theater, and dance. But how did they move from being ordinary to being truly extraordinary? We have much anecdotal evidence that indicates that this is a *choice*, a conscious decision whether to accept an ordinary state of complacency or discover one's greatness. We notice that many rather good and even talented people settle for being good enough. A mere few decide to navigate the uncharted waters of their full physical and spiritual human potential in order to experience new heights of personal performance, recognized as extraordinary levels of functioning.

Athletes like Michael Jordan, Lance Armstrong, and Tiger Woods are examples of ordinary humans who have discovered ways to break away from the masses and achieve extraordinary levels of functioning. They are ordinary in that they need strong determination, dedication, perseverance, and the deep desire to be the best they can be—they do not excel by magic. For example, Jordan always showed up for practice an hour before his teammates; Woods has been known to practice for two hours on the putting green following an intense eighteen holes; Armstrong suffered through workouts during extremely cold weather, knowing it made him a tougher competitor. All of these exemplary performers share a simple goal: to do the best they can to be the best they can be. This is the only goal that ultimately matters; from this, all is possible. This is because, as you will see, the heart overrides the ego (head) as the inner battles over fear, frustration, and self-doubt are won with warrior virtues such as courage, compassion, persistence, integrity, and selflessness. This is the warrior journey, the journey to the extraordinary.

EMPTINESS · The most recognizable symbol associated with Zen Buddhism is the circle, whose empty center represents infinite possibility and growth. We chose the circle for our cover art because it is such a fundamental concept of the book. Notice: the circle has no beginning and no end, yet it is complete, much like the warrior path itself. The circumference represents your journey as you adventure along, only to return to where you began more evolved, wiser, and more aware.

The shape of the circle, the letter *O*, represents oneness in relation to all things, every aspect of the journey—its ups and downs, setbacks and advances, yin and yang. In Chinese, this empty space is called *wu ji*, the fertile void of everlasting potential. It is a place of not knowing that enables you to fill up, to learn, grow, and improve along the warrior path toward the extraordinary.

You must not be fearful of not knowing. If your cup is full, nothing can enter; you learn nothing, and expansion ceases. Not knowing is liberating, as you emancipate yourself from ignorance and become free and limitless. Wu ji gently gives you permission to face your fears, vulnerabilities, and insecurities in a light, humorous fashion as you flow to the vast empty sea of possibility. Here is the open space of profound growth and change, where you learn to let go of the steering wheel. This idea of going forward while not knowing helps you create enormous internal strength and wisdom. Sometimes you must take a leap of faith and trust that you will either land on two feet or fly.

We ask that you let your heart and mind remain open to vast self-expansion as you continually maintain an empty mind, realizing how little you know and how much there is to learn. Warriors remain empty so that their learning curve remains steep. From this humble heart-space, the sky is the only limit. Sometimes, as an athlete, you have to unlearn all you have learned and be open to new and better ways. For example, a few years ago, Tiger Woods changed his swing at the suggestion of his coach in order to help his game get to a new level. At first it was difficult for him, but by being open to the possibilities, he began to improve, winning several consecutive major tournaments in the process. Old habits are not easy to unlearn, and you may feel frustrated and impatient at times, but with an open heart and mind, you become pregnant with exciting growth, change, and potential.

All the great performers in sports, fitness, martial arts, and dance embrace—albeit with some fear—the sacred space of emptiness, the eternal empty circle. Now, in your visualization of this concept, remember to feel the feeling of emptiness and remain open to possibilities. Feel yourself going forward on your path to success.

DECLARATION: I refuse to let my fear prevent me from staying open to change that will potentially propel me to the next level in my physical endeavors. I am empty and open to filling up for self-expansion.

REFLECTION: If I changed things, what specific aspects of my game could potentially expand my possibilities? What fears do I have about admitting that I don't know?

Gratefulness

GRATEFULNESS • How many of us arrive at the arena of performance with full minds and empty hearts? Minds filled with trivia, distraction, and minor details interfere with awareness and focus. In the grand scheme of life, what is truly important is this present moment: the breath that gives and sustains life, enabling you to perform. Zen is a practice of celebrating the present as you become conscious of what is genuinely important. The warrior's heart takes nothing for granted.

When you acknowledge the gifts of life and hold gratitude deep within, you are ready to perform with a clear mind and a focused heart.

Jerry often conducts the following exercise on gratefulness with his teams prior to an important practice or a game that needs to be played with high-level intensity and integrity.

Before you begin your workout, training session, or work for the day, think of seven aspects of life that you appreciate. For example, your skills, talents, mind, health, family, opportunities, and work. Now, with eyes closed, connect to the feeling of appreciation. Imagine this feeling coming into your body in three deep breaths, as each breath surrounds the heart. Hold each breath there as the feeling begins to expand. With this sensation of gratitude in the heart, make your performance today a reflection and extension of that appreciation.

Now, open your eyes and take on the day's tasks. If you are grateful and appreciative of your health, feel your vitality. If you are appreciative of your talents, be sure to use them consciously this day. If you have a great family, be certain you communicate: talk to them.

Notice the difference in how you perform. Such ordinary moments create the extraordinary in all you do.

DECLARATION: When I refuse to take things for granted and I focus on gratitude, I become aligned with my heart and connected to my performance.

REFLECTION: What are seven aspects of my life—the tangible and the intangible—that I truly appreciate? What does the act of identifying these do for me right now?

Commitment

COMMITMENT • Many people in sports and fitness are complacent, content with their level of accomplishment; they lack the desire to discover their true greatness. It's fine to be happy with your level of competency, but if you wonder why you remain stagnant, consider the notion of committing to higher levels and all that it may entail. Taking your performance to another, higher level demands the attitude of a warrior: the commitment of the heart to the journey from merely competent to superb. We encourage you to commit to doing all you can to be the best you can be, regardless of sacrifice or suffering. Zen teaches that suffering is the path to awareness. In sports, it's the way of the champion warrior and the path to greatness. And besides, doing anything at a higher level is simply more satisfying.

In athletics as well as other aspects of your life, your level of commitment is constantly being tested. Some of the more easily recognizable indicators that you have made a commitment to a certain path are these: you insist that you will not make excuses for marginal performance; you view your competitor as a partner to help bring out your best; you thirst for new ways to improve; you are eager to put forth extra effort when needed; you experience an absence of lingering doubt; you refuse to view discouragement and disappointment as anything but natural; you feel a natural and all-encompassing sense of joy and motivation to do all you can to be the best you can be.

The sky is the limit when you demonstrate a consistent, never-ending commitment to what you deeply desire and want to achieve. It is the main ingredient that separates ordinary performers from those who do extraordinary things. True commitment is devotion to a cause, an ideal, or a goal that may be more crucial than victory itself. German poet and philosopher Johann von Goethe once wrote: "Until one is committed, there is hesitancy, the chance to draw back ... there is one elementary truth, the ignorance of which kills countless ideas and splendid plans: that the moment one commits, then providence moves too. All sorts of things occur to help one that never would have occurred ... incidents, meetings and material assistance which no man could have dreamed would come his way."

Consider whether your lack of commitment is simple complacency or whether you might want to look deeper to see if there is another sport or activity that will engender a higher level of commitment. In other words, lack of commitment may be a sign that it's time to move on to something else that's more appropriate to your development at this particular time. Remember, too, that if your performance consistently falls short of your potential, you may lack commitment. Anything that is truly important to you in life is worthy of your full commitment.

DECLARATION: If I am to discover the next level of performance in my sport, fitness routine, and work, I must commit to doing even that which I do not wish to do.

REFLECTION: What do I need to commit to that will kick my performance up a notch? What is required in order to make that commitment happen?

HSING · In Chinese, *hsing* refers to the unity of heart and mind, their coming together to affirm nature's way, the way of the warrior. The calligraphic symbols depict a centered body-mind-spirit disposition with a fully expressive and blossoming heart.

Most of us view heart and mind as separate entities; the Spirit of the Dancing Warrior perceives them as a dynamic interaction aligned for extraordinary possibility. Training, competing, and working from a head-space creates obsession with outcomes, results, past mistakes, and future failures. This leads to anxiety and self-doubt. The warrior relishes and visualizes the thought of victory but also knows that the heart speaks in the moment for positive focus on the matter at hand, for controlling what one can with passion, fire, and energy.

For example, if you are a runner, you may want to win the race, get a good time for the distance, or place well in your age category. These are things you may want to *feel* through visualization in advance of your run. Then, when you show up for the event, simply come to compete and focus on the little things that make you feel good and run well—your stride, arm carriage, proper breathing, cadence. Let these propel you toward accomplishing your goal. In this way your body follows the heart in the moment. Not obsessing on outcomes will relax you and help you perform at higher levels.

A good example of this can be found in the games of golf and tennis. So many players obsess about the previous blunder—lipping a putt or double-faulting the serve—to such an extent that they become anxious, tense, and tentative at the very next opportunity. To bring the heart and mind together and be present in the moment, tell yourself the following: "That was lousy, but I can do better. Here I go." Then mentally correct the error and tell yourself: "Here it is, one stroke/point at a time. Here is a new beginning, a new opportunity to demonstrate great golf/tennis."

You can always begin again in this moment by using these kinds of affirmations to stay present. Unlike the past or future, this is something you can control. When heart and mind function in alignment as one, you seek the extraordinary each day, affirming your direction and efforts as you demonstrate integrity: doing what you say you'll do.

DECLARATION: My best performance is the result of the dynamic unity of heart and mind, where the mind cooperates with what the heart knows to be right. I cherish victory, yet create success in the process.

REFLECTION: What specifically can I do to assist myself in aligning my heart and mind, while enjoying the process and being in the moment?

Respect

RESPECT • The warrior is intent on demonstrating the virtue of respect—for self, teammates, coaches, and opponents. There are many ways of being disrespectful in sports: showing up late for practice, not learning the routines and plays, refusing to give your all, behaving inappropriately, yelling at others, using sarcasm, student-athletes not going to classes, failure to hustle, and more. Similar patterns can be found in the workplace or the home. Respect coincides with the Zen teaching *do the right thing*. Respect is really about developing relationships in an environment of integrity, positive communication, trust, loyalty, compassion, and dignity.

An attitude of respect is crucial in achieving high-level performance. We know of a collegiate women's basketball team that was talented, passionate, and united as a group yet could never realize its potential and win because the coaching staff was blatantly disrespectful and abusive, to each other as well as to the athletes. Sarcasm, shame, and foul language tore these great spirits apart, and their performance reflected this hostile environment. Healthy coach-athlete relationships are built on trust and loyalty through positive communication and forgiveness. The key is to respect all others as you would like to be respected.

Such is the case at the University of North Carolina's women's lacrosse program. Unlike the basketball team discussed earlier, the staff treat the Tarheel women very differently: in a firm yet healthy and fair manner. Jenny Levy, head coach, and her assistants interact with the athletes with the utmost unconditionally positive regard. They set the boundaries and enforce them firmly, yet do so with a great deal of respect. As a result, all parties perform at higher levels in their sport and in their lives generally.

In Chinese, the symbols for respect express the understanding that respect for others begins with respect for yourself.

Think of throwing a stone in the center of a pond and how every ripple reaching outward begins at the single point where the stone initially dropped in. In the same way, all respect for others begins first with self-respect. With such respect, you create an environment that is conducive to extraordinary performance. Respect is one aspect of love, and when an athlete feels respected and loved by a coach, he or she will go the distance—do what is asked and more. When you respect and love others, you don't lose power or control; you gain it. A lack of respect creates resistance, alienation, and resentment—even revolt.

According to the *I Ching*, the ancient Chinese book of change, respect of others creates a spirit of loyalty. Followers are motivated to take on hardship and sacrifice in the attainment of goals. Great coaches and leaders, such as our friend Phil Jackson of the Los Angeles Lakers, create environments that are trusting, open, and respectful. Jackson understands that he gains power by having respect for and listening to his athletes. They then mirror his behavior as they achieve high levels of performance. In your other roles in life, such as that of a CEO or a parent, you may have also discovered how respect creates the outcome you desire. In the case of parenting, what we notice is how cooperative our kids are when treated with respect. Listening with love and caring seems to mitigate rebellion in so many youngsters.

DECLARATION: When I demonstrate the heart-driven virtue of respect for myself and others, I create environments where great accomplishments are not only possible but inevitable. Success is the by-product of respect and love.

REFLECTION: Under what circumstances do I demonstrate a lack of respect for myself or others? What can I do to change that?

Partnership

PARTNERSHIP • The *I Ching* tells us "working together, the interaction of your spheres of influence can achieve significant deeds." We encourage you to relax and embrace and be thankful for your opponents, as they are your teachers who challenge you to reach heights you might never attain without them. True strength, like water, blends with opposing forces. A warrior does not view opponents as the enemy to be beaten or killed. Such thought patterns could cause you great stress and anxiety. Instead, remember that the word *competition* in Latin means "to seek together."

The two Chinese symbols for partnership depict the two partners seeking each other to achieve wholeness, to become one, sharing the same spirit and goal for achievement. Opponents become partners in the same dance. In all of your competitive events, consider your opponents as partners who help you seek greatness. A good warrior opponent is someone who will challenge you to discover your best. A Buddha buddy will push the pace on a run or bike ride and attack the hill with intent. This invites you to push beyond what you thought were limits. Whether working out or working on a corporate team, you achieve so much more by working together.

Take your inspiration from nature. Remember that flocks of geese flying in V formation travel 71 percent farther by helping each other. Other birds, when flying as partners, can travel as much as three thousand miles in four and a half days nonstop, rest for a few days, and then repeat the process.

DECLARATION: I love my opponent because the better the competition, the more I discover how good I really am. Competition always brings out the opportunity for personal-best performance.

REFLECTION: What might I gain or learn from viewing my opponent as my partner, mentor, or teacher? In what ways can I teach my opponent to take it up a notch?

Perseverance

PERSEVERANCE • The Chinese character for perseverance illustrates strength and unwavering groundedness in the spirit of the performer. When you handle suffering with a warrior's heart, eventual success will be your reward. Know that talent, as important as it is, accounts for a mere 5 percent of most achievements.

As you have no doubt experienced, performance can become discouraging. The warrior's heart enables you to be resilient, to get back up again and again—in a deliberate, intentional way—when you feel down. The Chinese sage Confucius encourages us to not lose heart until the task is complete through steadfast movement on the path to extraordinary performance.

When you are discouraged with the level of development of your physical skills, change your focus from outcomes and results to the joy of the process, the worthwhile experience of development itself, knowing that fulfillment will come if you stay on course.

In his beautiful, enchanting novel *The Alchemist*, Paulo Coelho writes a dazzling fable about how people on a journey across a vast desert get discouraged and quit just before palm trees appear on the horizon. When tested, they give up. *Spirit of the Dancing Warrior* reminds you to not let this happen in your life. "The warrior accomplishes significant deeds through enduring effort in a consistent direction," says the *I Ching*. The Buddha, we are told, is still only halfway to his destination but keeps going regardless. When you seem to be stuck, not making progress in any of life's endeavors, compassion may remind you that you are not alone; everyone experiences blockage and obstacles that discourage forward movement. Can you sense that the experience, the journey itself is worthwhile? Rather than letting them annoy you, see the plateaus you reach along the way as essential periods of deeper learning and mastery. Plateaus appear as a level of performance that recurs until the body establishes muscle memory and inner intelligence. Notice that despite all its twists and turns, the river eventually finds its way to the sea.

DECLARATION: With strength, steady movement, and consistent hope, I await the dawning of a new day. I expect good things to happen when I persevere.

REFLECTION: What examples do I have in my life about being ready to quit but choosing to persevere instead? What aspects of my present life could benefit from my willingness to persevere? What's stopping me from hanging in there?

WARRIOR • Traditionally, the warrior embraced war as a way of life, using swords to defeat the enemy. Today, the modern warrior fights inner battles with weapons of the heart, and his war is the effort to include the subtle aspects of spiritual self-mastery in his way of life. Here we provide guidance for such spiritual training and transpersonal development, with self-awareness as the cornerstone of growth and change.

The Buddha is the awakened one, and the warrior strives for such awakening through action, preferably of the physical kind. Action is only possible because the warrior has both the courage to fail and the compassion to heal. Failure is the teacher, emblematic of extraordinary possibility and free of regret in an environment where risk is the rule rather than the exception. Integrity is, perhaps, the most important trait of the warrior, who consistently lives by his word. Humility, loyalty, dignity, courtesy, intensity, perseverance, sacrifice, and suffering are some of the other elements that characterize the true warrior. In sports, being a warrior is not tied to winning; it means being in the process of competing and fighting, not for victory but for respect.

In athletics, the goal of the warrior is to do the best you can to be the best you can be. You position yourself for the possibility of victory within, against the inner demons of fear, failure, frustration, and self-doubt. Patience, diligence, and determination contribute to self-mastery. Ultimately, the warrior has no regrets as he walks away from the mat of life, journeying with heart as an indomitable spirit.

DECLARATION: My challenge in sports, fitness, and life is to practice the way of the warrior in pursuit of complete self-awareness and personal development.

REFLECTION: What can I do today to demonstrate the courage to take a risk in order to improve myself in sports, fitness, or life?

REFLECTION • All physical performance has its ups and downs, subject to the natural cycles of life. Periodic fluctuations in performance are sacred opportunities to reflect upon your relationship with sports, fitness, and life—their patterns and rhythms shift and change. The warrior understands life's patterns through reflection, asking, "Where have I been, where am I now, and where am I going?" The answers often lead to positive growth.

For the warrior, reflection is an inner voyage of exploring new ideas, new experiences, a new career or role. It is a time to question and reevaluate, to check in on how things are going with your sport or fitness regimen and perhaps your life as a whole. Reflection is a way to tune in to your body, mind, and spirit and assess your training and competitive performance.

Following battle, the samurai warrior would ask two important reflective questions: What went well? What needs work? For example, you can assess how well you competed with heart from the start and continued throughout the entire contest, or how the defense played beyond expectations. You can also discuss on-the-field communication that needs work. Apply this same evaluation process to your work and home. These penetrating and evaluative inquiries will carry you from affirming the good (went well) to a proactive approach to moving forward (needs work). Like a brave, indomitable warrior, refuse to ride the windowless train, traveling blindly only to get off at the last stop and wonder, "Where have I been? What was that all about?"

The *I Ching* says, "Your inner stillness and reflection bring enlightenment … you see situations in a strange new light."

DECLARATION: When I go inside, I can move outside. I will stop, look, and listen to the inner voice of reflection.

REFLECTION: Today, how do I feel physically, emotionally, and spiritually? Why? How do these feelings impact me going forward?

Compassion

COMPASSION • When two armies meet, the one with compassion is the one that tastes victory. These thoughts from the ancient Chinese sage Lao Tzu reflect the sentiments of legendary basketball coach Phil Jackson, who claims that without compassion, his Chicago Bulls would never have sustained such high levels of extraordinary excellence. The warrior understands that compassion ignites one's courage to take risks to excel because, regardless of outcomes or results, compassion will help you to endure hardship and setbacks.

Compassion for self as well as others gives you permission to fail—not that you would choose such a path. It creates safe, understanding environments—inner and outer—that encourage you to trust yourself, your team, coaches, coworkers, and friends to continue their efforts in the face of adversity. The warrior surges ahead of the pack following devastating defeats because he performs in a culture of compassion.

One of the most important virtues of Buddhism and Zen is compassion for ourselves and for other human beings. The Chinese symbols for compassion depict a generosity of the heart followed by an active eagerness to participate in the opponent's joy as well as sorrow. Whether in victory or defeat, compassion for self and others is the key to success in attaining true well-being. When you win an athletic contest, your Buddha-nature might ask, *How does my opponent feel right now?*

Immediately following and in the midst of celebrating their national championship in field hockey, the University of Maryland women's team paused and noticed their dejected opponents, the University of Michigan team, clearly feeling the agony of defeat. At that sensitive moment, the victors went to embrace and thank the runner-ups for their courageous and fearless battle and for playing all out with heart. This gesture took the sting out of the loss, and two years later, the University of Michigan went on to beat Maryland for the championship. *How does my opponent feel right now?* helps us keep our battles in perspective.

DECLARATION: Rather than be critical of myself or others, I choose to put my heart on the line and act with compassion and love.

REFLECTION: In what specific ways and under what circumstances can I demonstrate compassion to myself and my teammates? What do I imagine I will feel as a result of this from-the-heart approach? What effect could this have on my future performance?

PATIENCE • How does the tortoise defeat the hare? He uses the inner spiritual qualities of slow, steady, deliberate, patient movement. How does one eat an elephant? One bite at a time. So it is with sports, fitness, and life. Notice how all physical endeavors contain a natural flow. We know that rushing, forcing, or pushing for results often creates counterforces such as burnout, injury, setbacks, or failure. Doing too much too soon—that hurry-up syndrome—invariably leads to injury or illness, nature's built-in way of telling us to slow down and pause.

Simply put, whether you are an athlete, corporate worker, homemaker, or student of dance, take a day off from the routine. The pause is an essential aspect of high-level personal performance. We notice that when we become patient, we actually reach our goals sooner. We can do this when we immerse ourselves in the process, the flow of life, as it assumes its own form and shape, rather than forcing things to be what we think they should be.

Would you ever go into the garden, walk over to the daisies, and attempt to pull them upward to hasten their growth? Of course not. So why would anyone try to interfere with the natural growth and development of any physical or intellectual endeavor? For all of us, improvement in any experience always occurs not when we think it should, but when the time is right. This is when we are at our best. Warrior wisdom says: when you hasten the natural process, setbacks will occur. Your awakened Buddha self can enjoy the process, slow down, and arrive sooner; the journey is often the best part. Focus your heart-mind in the present and realize that the moment you have been waiting for is already here. Taoist philosopher Lao Tzu encourages patience and reminds us how all things occur at the appropriate time. Things happen not when we think they should but when we are ready. So slow down and arrive sooner.

DECLARATION: I am willing and eager to be at peace with the natural unfolding of my abilities. I refuse to place time constraints on my perfect progress.

REFLECTION: Why is it so important for me to force or try to make situations in my life happen more quickly than they naturally do? How will being impatient cause the plane to leave on time? How will it hasten the accomplishment of any endeavor?

FORTITUDE • We know that continuous, consistent strength and high-level performance are not possible. You may want to always be your best, look good, and be fast, but no one is capable of this all the time, not even the Buddha. During down times—times of strife, loss, setbacks, mistakes, uncertainty, and disappointment—the warrior adopts the virtue of fortitude, a sense of quiet inner strength, trust, and confidence, closely aligned with the warrior virtue of perseverance, that helps one to endure. We know from our own experience that this virtue will help you through a slump, a losing streak, an injury, or a disappointing result.

For the warrior, fortitude is a strong spiritual weapon that helps fight the inner wars of fear and self-doubt. It has helped nations throughout the world to survive amid devastation. Native American Lakota culture, for example, survives thanks to its strongest weapon, fortitude. This warrior virtue has won world wars. It is the virtue that gets you through the moment, that enables you to endure shock and disappointment. Parents who discover that their child has a fatal disease, athletes who sustain a season-ending injury, workers who lose their jobs in a tough economy: these are all examples of situations requiring fortitude, which helps those enduring such adversity to live one moment at a time. At its foundation are a quiet confidence and a deep belief that everything will work out. Think of bamboo and how it bends in a windstorm, yet survives. Fortitude, or bravery, is your ability to bend and dance in the wind of adversity—on and off the court and in and out of the gym, boardroom, or living room—and bounce back on your feet, hold your head up, and go forward. We call this dance the "Buddha Bounce."

DECLARATION: I am brave and strong enough to endure all setbacks and adverse conditions. I have the courage and confidence to continue on the path and realize my true potential.

REFLECTION: In what specific ways can I apply the concept of fortitude to my present physical and emotional life? Whom do I know and respect who demonstrates this warrior virtue and in what way?

HUMOR • One of the greatest mistakes you can make is to think of the spiritual training in this book as deadly serious. Perhaps more than any other spiritual tradition, Zen Buddhism teaches us how to bring out our sense of humor. When you find yourself lost in a frowning cosmic space, take the s out of *cosmic* and laugh at your cheerless sobriety.

Many of us on a physical, emotional, and spiritual path take ourselves too seriously. If you run, bike, swim, or partake in any other exhausting activity, notice what happens and how you feel when you change your frown from the pain of exertion to a smile. Instantly, you are transformed: your body relaxes and the activity seems painless. When you are tired and hurting, picture the Happy Buddha, his belly shaking with laughter as if filled with jelly. In Chinese, laughter is depicted as a person with arms and legs flung wide open, head to the sky, vibrating with mirth like bamboo leaves in the wind. In Zen, the ability to laugh at ourselves and experience the humor in our mistakes and foibles is an indication of self-awareness and consciousness.

When your performance falls short of your high expectations, your ego interferes and you feel embarrassed by such setbacks. You begin to measure your self-worth as an athlete, performer, or person by your mistakes, errors, and failures. You may instead want to create expectations that are more process than product oriented. For example, expect to do well, have fun, and allow good things to happen. Rather than dwell on the darkness, affirm your efforts to be your best; affirm your health and the opportunities given to you and your friends. Laugh, knowing that after all, you are an imperfect, vulnerable, and sometimes silly human being.

The ancient Taoist masters always managed to check their own follies with a practice of letting their long knotted hair down and sticking out their bellies, roaring with laughter when they fumbled. Imagine great athletes and world leaders laughing Buddhalike when they stumble over their serious work. When they see the humor in it and don't take themselves too seriously, they usually begin to perform at higher levels. Humor relaxes the body, mind, and spirit and, as we know, this has the effect of improving outcomes.

DECLARATION: While I take what I do seriously, I refuse to attach my ego to the outcomes. I choose to laugh when I blunder.

REFLECTION: Why might some people think of spirituality as a serious experience? In retrospect, when have I taken myself too seriously and how would I handle that today?

Part II: Preparation
From Buddha to Bob Marley

In this, the second stage along the path of the Spirit of the Dancing Warrior, we shift gears to preparing and focusing our minds on positive, productive thought. In the words of the Buddha, "Our lives are shaped by our minds; we become what we think." When our thoughts become destructive, negative, or counterproductive, they trap us. Bob Marley, in his superb classic "Redemption Song", makes the point that we all must work to find avenues to escape mental incarceration because if we don't no one else will and our lives will forever be bound by limited mind-sets.

There is one consistent difference between a poor performance and a very good one: your thoughts. For example, if your thoughts are focused on what you cannot control—results, time, points, or goals scored—you become tense and tentative, and you create much self-doubt. Your performance will invariably be disappointing. On the other hand, shift your focus to what you can control—the process, the little things, the preparation, the effort, your mental state—and you will become relaxed and confident, and your performance will be quite satisfying. Where the mind goes, so goes your performance. Change your thoughts and watch your life change.

The good news is that you are in charge. Thoughts are only thoughts, and you get to choose between those that hinder and those that help. In this, the second stage of our journey, we will help you prepare your mind with positive, forward-moving thoughts and words that are specifically associated with the mental and spiritual mechanics of performance. If and when negative thoughts come into your head, simply say, "Thank you. Good-bye." Acknowledge them and invite them to leave.

THOUGHT • You may notice how random thoughts seem to enter the conscious mind quite suddenly and for no apparent reason. They can be positive or negative, and those that predominate are the ones you feed, or give the most attention to. To better handle your thoughts—to use the positive ones to best effect and keep those that are not helpful from acquiring power and throwing a shadow over your life—it is best to identify them as they appear. The idea is to recognize constructive thoughts and to creatively use them to your advantage while disregarding those that disturb.

As described earlier in the book, meditation and affirmation are effective ways to help you focus on positive thinking. Who you are, what you do, and where you go are the direct result of your thoughts. They can either strengthen you or weaken you. In sports, fitness, and other physical activities, your performance is shaped by your mind; you become what you think. For example, let's say a tennis player gets unraveled after hitting a lousy shot. Her thoughts are: "I stink. What's wrong with me? I can't win." These words create self-doubt, and she begins to play tentatively out of fear of losing. If instead she says to herself: "Yeah, that was an awful shot, but I can do better. I'm a strong, elite athlete. Here I go," her more positive, proactive affirmation would guide her to resume playing in a more focused, confident way.

When you change your thoughts, your performance follows. When you are running up a hill, lifting weights, or executing an advanced ballet move, notice the difference in how you feel when you think, "I can do it—I am strong" versus "I can't do it—I'm a wimp." Shifting between negative and positive thoughts creates a subsequent shift in your capabilities. When evaluating your performance, rather than focusing on negative thinking—"What went wrong?"—first ask yourself "What went well?" and follow that question with "What needs work?" These two queries are proactive thoughts that create forward movement and confidence. Remember Bob Marley's outlook: we are all responsible for our own mental freedom. Ask yourself: Is my glass of thoughts half empty or half full?

DECLARATION: I choose to think positively and ask, Why not? I change my performance by focusing on possibilities, not disabilities.

REFLECTION: What are five situations in my life in which I stand in my own way by being negative? What can I do today to change my related, hindering thoughts?

Beginner's Mind

BEGINNER'S MIND • Shunryu Suzuki, in his classic work *Zen Mind, Beginner's Mind*, writes, "In the beginner's mind there are many possibilities; in the expert's mind, there are few." There is a tremendous advantage to be gained by clearing your mind through meditation and then focusing your attention on the possibilities awaiting you. Don't let preconceived biases prevent you from being attuned to your human potential.

In 1954, Roger Bannister broke the four-minute barrier in the mile run, which the experts considered impossible at the time. Yet within the next year and a half, over fifty athletes around the world ran it in under four minutes. They could now see the possibility and were open to doing what was required to reach that once "impossible" level of performance.

The warrior's mind is a beginner's mind, one that is open, receptive, and nonjudgmental; with this mind, all is possible. We want to encourage you to follow Bannister and challenge your beliefs, seeing them as limits and going beyond them. For example, you might say, "It could never happen," or, "I'm not strong enough, fast enough, good enough." Start to notice how these words limit you, and then with a beginner's mind, turn such statements around. Say, "I can do it—I am strong," as you try to run up that hill or lift that weight.

When you're feeling stuck in failure, loss, or setback, take the Spirit of the Dancing Warrior new beginnings approach, in which you give yourself permission to start again fresh. After a poor golf shot, for instance, approach the next shot and say to yourself, "Here is a new beginning, a chance to start again—every shot is an opportunity to demonstrate my greatness." If you're playing in a soccer game, come out in the second half and play as if the score is zero-zero, even if the other team is up. Use this beginner's mind-set to increase your chances to experience the extraordinary.

DECLARATION: The more I develop the beginner's mind and remain open to possibilities by questioning limits, the more I perform freely to play up to my capacity.

REFLECTION: What are three of my most powerful limiting beliefs, and what can I do to change them and go beyond them? What is possible if I free myself to play to my capacity? What do I need to do to accomplish this?

INNER STILLNESS • We would like to gently remind you to hold firm to inner stillness. You cannot see your image in running water, but you can in water that is at rest. In our work, we teach that meaningful, extraordinary performances are the by-product of inner stillness. Outer movement in your life is enhanced by quiet within, particularly during times of frustration, disappointment, and crisis.

The Chinese symbols for inner stillness represent the inner peace attained by being at ease with the calmness and clarity experienced when not striving. How you handle your body in sports and during other physical activity is directly related to, and a function of, such stillness. For example, when you focus on outcomes or results, when you show up to win instead of simply to compete, everything gets thrown off. Lose the still place, lose the race. Your performance must revolve around this inner calm within.

Scholar and world-class athlete Joseph Campbell talks about this still place in *The Hero's Journey*. An amazing 800-meter runner, he knew that he had lost two important races because he lost that still point. The races were so important to him that he focused on winning instead of the process of simply running. As he put it, "The whole thing got thrown off." He was too concerned about outcome.

Winning a race, a match, a game, a contract, or a debate is always the manifestation of a calm, inner stillness and a focus on the process you are engaged in itself. Otherwise you get thrown off center and lose your chi; as a result, performance suffers. This is all about a subtle but powerful shift of focus from head to heart. You can facilitate this shift by taking some time to watch the breath as we described earlier in the book and by using visualization, feeling how you wish to feel prior to an activity and then carrying this quiet state and those feelings into the arena. Stop, look inside, and listen to your inner voice.

Take time to be still; there is no need to gallop on a wild horse through life. Get off your bike occasionally and admire the flowers. Contemplate the natural rhythms and cycles of the journey. Be in the *now*!

DECLARATION: My stillness sets in motion the easing of commotion. I control my still point by quieting the mind prior to performance and by focusing on the process, not the outcome.

REFLECTION: When have I experienced this feeling of inner stillness, and what seemed to contribute to it? What are the ways in which I can experiment with and apply this feeling today?

BELIEF • Your opponent's greatest advantage is your lack of belief in yourself. We have noticed how so many struggle with this. And although this struggle makes sense, they take believing in themselves to mean belief in winning or controlling results, neither of which is possible. But when your focus shifts to what you *can* control, the essential little things that add up to a great deal—your preparation, your attitude, your efforts in the process—your confidence begins to rise, self-doubt diminishes, and belief becomes a possibility.

The warrior believes that ultimate triumph is defined as the eagerness to be the best one can be by doing the very best one can do. With this as your goal, you garner belief in yourself as you call to mind all your accomplishments, skills, and talents that have created excellence in your past performances. Perhaps you can also believe in your teammates, coaches, and trainers—and be confident that they have your best interests in mind.

Researchers in the science of aviation have proven that the bumblebee is a terrific aviator, yet it is too small, too heavy, and too fat to fly. Yet it believes it can. Like this creature, you have inside you all that you need to get it done. Believe and receive. Sammy Davis Jr. transcended all racial and social barriers to become one of the most successful entertainers and showmen in the world. He always believed in his potential as a performer. The title of his autobiography, *Yes I Can*, tells it all.

DECLARATION: When I focus on the process and all that I bring to the arena—both my tangibles and intangibles—I begin to believe I can get the job done. I believe in my ability to execute because of my diligent and consistent preparation.

REFLECTION: What are all those essential little things that I can count on demonstrating during my event or activity? What can I control and how do I execute that brilliantly?

GOALS • Goals are like beacons, flashing lights on the horizon that keep you on track during a satisfying and rewarding journey. They shine in the distance, encouraging movement toward the extraordinary. For many athletes, setting goals in the traditional way creates tension, anxiety, and pressure as the focus shifts from the process to outcomes and results. We invite you to instead set lofty goals and dream about their realization, then pull back and enjoy being in the moment and involved in doing all the little things that are necessary to keep you on target. If you should fall short, you will still have achieved more than if your focus had been shortsighted.

The key to success with goals is to remember not to measure your self-worth by any outcome. Let your goals function as that distant lighthouse, guiding you from afar to move and perform in the present moment, one day at a time, and see how close you can get to fulfilling them.

The warrior way means setting your goals in the spirit of passion, aligning them with what you love, and then enjoying your movement and progress toward the lantern you have set to illuminate your way. For the potter, the treasure is not found in the finished pot but in the experience of making it. For the marathoner, the real prize is not the completion of the race but the dynamic three months of training that precede it. In the Asian art of archery, the archer focuses on the true bull's-eye, the dantien or gut center of his physical and emotional being, as he releases the arrow. If he is truly centered and his goal is to be the best he can be (the real target), he will experience success no matter where the arrow lands. The real target is within, and the achievement of the external goal is a mere reflection of his hitting this inner bull's-eye.

DECLARATION: I am able to set lofty, passionate goals because they enable me to achieve greater heights as I refuse to measure my self-worth by outcomes. My goals are lanterns that light the way.

REFLECTION: Following the Spirit of the Dancing Warrior way, what goals am I now willing to establish so I can position myself for extraordinary growth? What do I gain from this new way of setting goals?

FOCUS • The *Tao Te Ching* says, "Hold on to the ancient Tao, control the current reality." In other words, when you stay focused in the moment, you control what can be controlled— you take charge. Such was the case of a world-class athlete who, running a marathon, told his tired body not to run twenty-six miles; he told it to run one mile and repeat it twenty-six times. His focus was on one small segment at a time. Small, manageable segments offer a way to focus on each step of the way, whether in an athletic event or any other area of life. This will both relax and energize you while also increasing your confidence in achieving the task as you control your current reality.

Focus is the calm state of parking your attention on your experience in the moment rather than on past events or future possibilities. This Zen state is equivalent to where your mind goes during a compelling movie or book as all else fades into the background. Many sports and fitness activities, such as swimming, running, hiking, dancing, and cycling, provide the chance to directly access this mental-emotional state in which mind and body function as a unit. For example, while swimming, focus simply on pulling water with each stroke; in cycling, focus on drawing circles with each revolution of the crank; focus on hand position while dancing; attend to the cadence while running.

We know that the difference between a good performance and a bad one in athletics and other physical activity is simply focus. So where must your focus lie? On what you can do in the moment. When your attention is on outcomes, results, or scores, which you can't control, you get tense and tentative, and your performance will usually suffer. When you focus instead on what you can control—the process, the little things, your attitude, the mechanics, and your mental training—you become calm, relaxed, and confident and thus create favorable results. Using meditation, visualization, and affirmation as suggested in this book will train your mind to have the focus of the warrior.

DECLARATION: I choose to focus only on what I can control, in that moment, and enjoy the process of experiencing my very best performances.

REFLECTION: What are all the little things involved in my physical activity that I can control, and how can I develop better focus in other parts of my world?

INSTINCT • The *I Ching* reminds us to "act out the dance of your inner self, trust the inherent correctness of your instincts ... in this way you will meet with success." Over the years, we have learned that to know and to act are one and the same. Your actions and performance are the result of the body's innate intelligence, coupled with a mind that trusts what the body knows while being willing to step out of the body's way. It is a response that comes from our unconscious minds. Martial artists call it a sixth sense, a state of hyper-awareness that produces calm in an otherwise fearful, tense situation. In sports, fitness, and life, performance is directly related to your ability to follow your instincts: those impulses, feelings, and automatic responses—quick reactions to fast-paced situations.

All great athletes trust their instincts: Tiger Woods, LeBron James, Kobe Bryant, and Roger Federer are just a few who have learned to do this. Whether anticipating a fastball, knowing when to surge in a race, positioning yourself to catch a pass, or reacting to defense or offense, you need to call upon and trust your intuitive self.

We all possess this instinct, yet few of us trust it to the extent we must to be successful. When we are in the midst of physical activity, there is often no time to think, so cultivate and develop your instincts as you practice and work out. Follow your inner voice and notice how things develop. Know that good things happen when you rely on natural insight.

Instinct, or intuitive action, is a significant aspect of Zen and Buddhist thinking, and having a Buddha mind means trusting and acting accordingly. Notice how your greatest successes occur during those times when you trust the wisdom of your heart, your basic instinct. Remember these words of the *Tao Te Ching*: "Evolved individuals know without going about, recognize without looking, achieve without acting."

DECLARATION: My instincts are the result of real knowledge, based on the wisdom gained from my experience. My performance success is the result of trusting and following this inner sixth sense. I am in sync with instinct.

REFLECTION: What recent success have I had using my instinct? In the future, what specific things can I do in situations I may envision that will allow me to trust and follow my instinct?

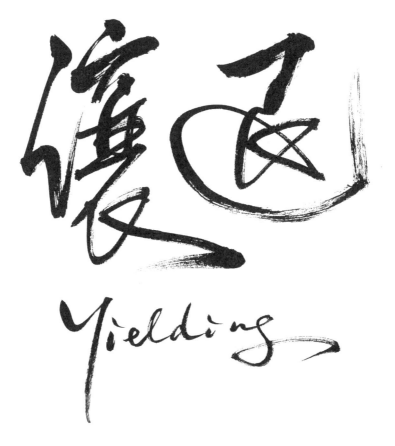

YIELDING · The Chinese symbols for yielding depict the way rivers and streams form their paths according to the dictates of nature: they yield to what is. Did you know that yielding conquers the resistant, and that soft triumphs over hard? Water is soft, yet wears away rock. Bamboo trees flex in the wind, flourish in the harsh winter, and are used to make shelter, while rigid pine trees crack during a storm.

Resistance to unpredictable change is pointless. We understand that we must yield to opposing forces by adapting to change. Flexibility and spontaneity are the keys to success in all arenas of physical activity. For example, in the martial arts, yielding to opposing forces is crucial; you absorb an attack by blending with its force. This is also true in football when an offensive lineman uses the force of the opposition to his advantage by stepping aside and taking his opponent to the ground. Yield to loss, yield to injury, yield to all conflict by being fluid, flexible, and soft.

Any changes in the normal routine of a game, event, or workout demand that you be flexible and yield. You may find yourself feeling angry and frustrated because you can't run due to unfortunate injury or weather obstacles. Can you try another source of exercise, perhaps cross-train on a bike or elliptical machine or swim in a pool? These are other ways in which you can still meet your needs of exercise. Such is the mental advantage you will have over those who remain psychologically rigid or resistant.

Rigidity causes tension and stress, which obstruct one's potential. We recall the story of a drunken man who falls off a cart without injury because he yields to the fall in a flexible, soft way. The wise warrior demonstrates true strength by yielding to sudden change, on or off the court. In his classic book on strategy and conflict resolution, *The Art of War*, Sun Tzu tells us to be creative and refuse to give preconceived notions permission to distract us from a powerful option—yielding.

When facing sudden and unpredictable change, adapt with flexibility. According to the wisdom of the East, those who are inflexible descend; the yielding will ascend.

DECLARATION: When I am inflexible and rigid, I set myself up for defeat. When I yield, I am in harmony with success.

REFLECTION: In what one way can I demonstrate the virtue of yielding today? What examples of rigidity do I have in my own past behavior, and how might I change them knowing what I know now?

CENTERED · We like to tell the story of a very talented potter whose creations are inconsistent. The quality of her work is directly related to the events in her life. If they throw her off center, her pottery becomes asymmetrical. When she remains centered and inwardly calm, she throws balanced, beautiful pottery.

To be centered is to perform up to your capabilities, regardless of what life throws your way. An athlete making a foul shot to win the game is centered when he or she is unfazed by the enormous distraction the opponent's fans are delivering. Athletics, fitness, and other physical activities provide a splendid opportunity to learn the delicate virtue of centeredness, the ability to block out distraction and quickly respond to unpredictable change when it occurs: noise, weather variation, unfair judgment calls, or any other unexpected situations that may arise.

Like a deeply rooted tree, centered people, like the potter or the athlete shooting a foul shot, remain unmoved by negative forces. Whenever you are confronted by external aggression or negative internal voices in your athletic life, understand that these forces are lessons your sport has offered you that help you shine in life itself.

The awakened person knows that victory and defeat are natural consequences of all performance situations. Refuse to go overboard in celebrating the former or brooding over the latter. The warrior enjoys the contest for what it truly is: a process of self-learning and mastery, which is defined as staying on track. Know that you will fall off track. Being truly centered simply means being able to return to that sacred place more quickly than before. We encourage you to meditate and then visualize yourself responding effectively to change or upheaval in your athletic, fitness, and performance life.

DECLARATION: Like a deeply rooted tree, I remain centered and free. I refuse to give anyone or anything permission to take me off center.

REFLECTION: Recall various situations in which you were caught off guard and lost your composure. What could you do to respond more appropriately to similar situations in the future?

FEAR • The warrior knows that fear is nature's way of helping one remain alert. It is a survival instinct that invites you
to assess a situation with caution prior to moving forward and
allows you to prepare for it properly. The *I Ching* tells us, "All
things in the cosmos will be aroused to movement through
fear. Cautious movement will bring success."

Approach fear as if it is a friend to acknowledge and embrace. To fight this natural emotion is to create a counterforce

that makes you tense and anxious, which interferes with performance. Fear is healthy. Listen to your fear as you descend down a steep, wet hill on your bike or attempt to dive off a forty-foot cliff into a lake, never having done it before.

Some tasks create fear because of their enormous scale. As an awakened one, you wisely divide them into small, manageable segments until you have completed them. Giving yourself permission to take one step at a time often reduces the intimidation and fear of an overwhelming situation.

According to the Tao, this approaching fear as a friend is the principle of *wu wei*, a way of working with fear by blending with its own force. Wu wei is effortless action, whereby you accept the natural way (it's natural to have fear) and exert the least amount of energy possible when faced with such a situation. Don't fight fear or try to run away from it. Listen to its message so you can make adjustments.

Realize, however, that sometimes fear is not fear, but an obsession with outcomes that cannot be controlled. Therefore, remember this: FEAR stands for False Evidence Appearing Real. If you feel you are in danger, ask yourself why you feel that way. Have you prepared well? Do you have all the information you need? Are you out of your comfort zone? Assess the situation and decide what to do.

We like to remember the words of philosopher-author Alan Watts: "The other side of every fear is freedom." Examine the fear and emancipate yourself from its grip. Once you discern what it is all about, you may discover that it is irrational; then you become free to transcend it and learn what is really possible. And remember, every warrior—and every athlete on every level—feels fear. As an athlete you must learn to be unafraid of fear and take the risks the journey toward the extraordinary entails.

DECLARATION: When I examine my fears, I learn to move cautiously forward. Fear is my friend; it is a healthy sign that I am alert to its message. Thank you, fear, for helping me here ... and for helping me hear your voice.

REFLECTION: What is the worst-case scenario if I don't listen to my fear? Can I live with the outcome? Am I well prepared for the task? Am I well informed? Well equipped?

Failure

FAILURE · It never feels good to lose, experience setbacks, make mistakes, or fail. Having had much failure in our lives, we notice that although it may cause disappointment at the time, all that we are today is the result of learning from such experiences. The warrior understands that, in this way, when we lose, we also win.

Lao Tzu failed, yet he knew that his failure was his best teacher, mentor, and guide. If you notice and pay attention to the way of the Buddha while in the gym or on the trail, you will learn that the arrow that hits the bull's-eye is the result of a hundred misses. Any of us who have become proficient with the computer in this technological age realizes that such skill is the result of errors, setbacks, and mistakes. As authors, we learn to write books by rewriting them.

We have worked closely with thousands of performers and with national champions in several sports, and we can say unequivocally that they have a very high tolerance for loss, setback, and failure. They would rather not have these experiences, but they know they are inevitable, and when they do occur, the best performers get back on their feet, learn from them, and become even greater because of their failure. Basketball icon Michael Jordan says, "I've missed more than nine thousand shots in my career; twenty-six times I've been trusted to take the game-winning shot and missed. I've failed over and over and over again. And that is why I succeed." Failure, for the warrior, is an opportunity for future success. We can tell you from working closely with many, many athletes that success comes to those who weather the storm.

DECLARATION: Failure is nature's way of teaching me how to improve. It is an important component of the process of living. Adversity gives me inner strength for another day.

REFLECTION: Look at your most recent failures, setbacks, and losses and ask yourself: What have I learned from these disappointing moments? How am I better off because of such failure?

Success

SUCCESS • Most of us have been raised in a society that measures success by outcomes and results: win the title, beat your opponent, dominate others, score goals, get hits. Good results are fun, but since we have no control over outcomes, attempting to control what we can't leads to a buildup of fear, anxiety, stress, tension, and self-doubt. When instead, like a warrior, you begin to focus on what can be controlled—doing the little things like keeping your eye on the ball, attending to physical mechanics, improving your attitude, feeling the experience, getting rest, eating well, and hydrating—you remain relaxed and confident.

When the archer shoots for the love of shooting, he has access to all his skills; when he shoots for gold, he blinds himself. We define success as the brilliant execution of all the little things rather than the marginal execution of all the brilliant things. An ancient Asian adage says: "From little streams come big rivers." When you achieve solid success in what you can control, the outcome is often success on the scoreboard of athletics, fitness, and life. We all love positive outcomes, and the satisfaction of reaching goals—success of that kind feels good. But we must remind ourselves that those happy outcomes are usually the by-product of the process. This helps us to detach from results and succeed no matter the outcome of our efforts.

DECLARATION: I refuse to give outcomes and results permission to detract from my mission: I will be successful in controlling what I can, and the rest will take care of itself.

REFLECTION: What are five little things about my sport, fitness program, or physical activity that, if I execute them, will lead me to experience success and enjoy the process?

EXPECTATIONS • Regardless of your level of participation in sports or fitness programs, your performance will invariably be influenced by your expectations of results. Should you expect a particular outcome? The samurai warrior would tell you: "Expect nothing, but be ready for anything." This advice sounds counterintuitive, but in our experience, we have found this concept to be quite helpful.

Do you know the difference between a good performance and a bad one (or a good day and a bad day)? It's very simple: good performances always happen when you have no expectations, let your activity unfold, and trust things will work out. You can then relax and focus on the series of actions you will carry out, the little things you can control. Bad performances, on the other hand, happen when you try to control the end result and have high expectations. Trying to control what you can't—the finished product—causes anxiety and tension.

The Chinese symbols for expectation show the enjoyment of someone watching the rising and setting of the moon in its natural arc across the sky. In Taoist thinking, if you can flow with nature's organic process as you enjoy your work fully in the moment, you will truly be fulfilled and you will feel successful in everything you do. If you must expect something, we remind you that if you prepare well and execute all the little things brilliantly, you can *expect* good things to happen, that you will do well and experience personal satisfaction and joy from your performance. "But I want to win," you say. You will win *if you refuse to expect to win*. Think about it! Know this: if you let go of the need to win, you will be victorious. Now, this idea is very Zen, but also very true.

DECLARATION: I focus on my preparation and the process of executing my performance plan; therefore I can expect the best to happen, whatever it may be.

REFLECTION: Thinking about my past performances, what expectations did I have and how did they affect the outcome? What expectations am I holding on to for a future performance, and how are they impacting my focus and my nervous system?

PERFECTION • The Chinese symbols for perfection are about feeling contented, fulfilled, and completely in awe of the beauty of nature and its transformative variations in everyday living. Of course we want to continually improve and rise above our current level of skill, but in order to grow, we must know that wherever we are and however we feel, the moment is already perfect. We must always enjoy this perfection as we grow and evolve. At the same time, we must appreciate the concept of perfection as the living process of enjoying the essence of now. The warrior strives to enjoy the now by focusing on excellence, not perfection. Psychologist Carl Jung wrote: "Perfection belongs to the gods; the most we can hope for is excellence."

There are two kinds of athletes: those who fail and those who will fail. It is called the law of inevitability. Things come and go; you're up, then down; you win, then lose—these are the natural cycles of life. Even the greatest of the great are imperfect. Several of the top PGA golfers in the recent Masters Tournament in Augusta, Georgia, for example, missed putts within four feet of the hole over and over again. The best NBA stars miss free throws and lose games. Baseball greats have their batting slumps. NFL receivers drop balls in the end zone as time runs out. Everyone is perfectly imperfect.

It has been said that the Buddha is only halfway there. Wow! Where are *we* if this is so? We can assure you that your effort to be perfect is a setup for failure. It makes you tense, tight, and tentative: all conditions that inhibit your performance. Let go of external rewards, others' opinions, fear of failure, harsh self-criticism, dwelling on negative outcomes, and procrastination. These are all indicators of perfectionist tendencies. Refuse to give in to these tendencies, and align with the Tao, which says, "Yielding triumphs over the rigid." By being less rigid about results while releasing the irrational quest to be perfect, you reduce anxiety and stress and, ironically, your performance becomes more aligned with what you believe to be perfect. We suggest that you focus your energy in the here and now and on one goal: to do your best today in order to be the best you can be. In this way, you position yourself for extraordinary—if not perfect—performance.

DECLARATION: My performance can never be perfect, as perfection is an illusion, something unattainable. Instead, I strive for doing my best and let the by-product be excellence.

REFLECTION: Have I ever had a perfect performance in my life? In what situations do I seek perfection, and how, specifically, can I set things up so that I am not measuring my self-worth by outcomes?

WINNING • The decision to win is yours. You don't become a winner; you decide whether or not to live your daily life as a winner. The warrior makes a commitment each day to be a winner on the journey toward extraordinary performance. And understand, you can be a winner even if it's not reflected on the scoreboard or in the boardroom. Actually, being a true warrior has more to do with taking wise risks, failing, and getting back up to try again than it does with winning or victory. We encourage you to let go of the obsessive desire to produce or possess, and focus instead on the joy, the dance, the flow. The victory is in the moment, now, as you play.

In his classic work, *The Zen of Running*, Fred Rohé speaks the language of the warrior: "There are no possible victories except the joy you are living while dancing your run; you are not running for some future reward—the real reward is now!" Know that real winning is in the fun of executing a good, positive plan. When you free yourself from the need to win, you can focus on the process and increase the chances of victorious results. Dream about winning if you like, but show up to simply perform well. Let the possibility of a scoreboard victory guide you to being a winner every day. A Buddhist mind might be detached from winning and outcomes, but it enjoys the fruits of labor when they appear. It's fun to win, as you might imagine if you watched the Los Angeles Lakers celebrate their *fifteenth* world championship in 2009. These mature men were frolicking with joy in their locker room like a bunch of little kids.

DECLARATION: Winning is the rewarding journey, not the destination. Victory is transitory, but outstanding performances are not. I am a winner regardless of the outcome.

REFLECTION: What contributes to my feeling like a winner regardless of results? What might I do today that will help me to feel like a winner? What are some specific rewards I can receive during my performance?

Part III: Integration
From Thinking Body to Dancing Mind

In 1992, we coauthored our very first book, titled *Thinking Body, Dancing Mind*. Today it remains our perennial bestseller, has been published in seven languages, and continues to draw the attention of performers of all ages at all levels and in every arena of life, all around the globe.

The title is a provocative Eastern paradox. After all, doesn't the mind think and the body dance? Normally this is so, but the norm disregards the importance of body and mind working together to form a unified whole. Prevailing thought creates the illusion that they are separate entities, each doing its own thing, when in actuality they need to be in harmony; there must be a vital, simultaneous integration in order for extraordinary behavior and performance to occur.

Let us explain further. After much practice with any skill, the body develops what we call *innate intelligence*; it learns and then knows what to do and how to do it. The mind, however, can (and often does) sabotage with its thoughts the body's efforts to perform. It sends fearful, critical, and negative messages that are contrary to what the body is capable of doing. In this way, the mind becomes out of sync with the body, sending such erroneous messages as "I can't do this" or "I hate running hills," which impede the body from doing what it has been trained to do. What is needed, then, is for the mind to dance with the innately intelligent body by cooperating and affirming, "I can do it. I am strong." When this happens, your mind and body become integrated and create one unified, harmonious whole, resulting in extraordinary performance. At this point, you become your body; your body is you. Being your body is the third phase of the Spirit of the Dancing Warrior journey. Let's begin this integration now.

BEGINNINGS • Whether you are starting a simple fitness regimen, training to run a marathon, building a corporate team, or establishing a functional family, completing the task can seem a daunting proposition. Begin everything you find challenging to do by taking the first step; then follow up with another step, then another. It helps emotionally and mentally to break any new task up into small, manageable segments.

You need to train your body to run five miles and incrementally increase the mileage gradually until someday, a twenty-six-mile race seems plausible. After all, if the grandfather clock knew how many times it had to tick in its lifetime, it might have quit a long time ago. Lao Tzu reminds us that the journey of a thousand miles begins with single step.

Don't be concerned with how far or how quickly you travel at the beginning. Everyone's path is different, and you must understand this. The warrior knows that what matters from the outset is moving in a positive direction; make sure this is the direction your feet are pointed.

Begin a journey in athletics, fitness, or life, and never give up until you have reached the end. Through steadfast perseverance, you will attain success. To help with this, focus on the joy of the journey rather than the goal. Even as you struggle—and we all do—begin to see the value in this natural aspect of the journey. The struggle is teaching you something valuable about yourself, and when you complete the task, having stayed on course throughout the hard times, you exponentially increase your joy, satisfaction, and appreciation for what you have accomplished. The experience itself becomes the primary purpose of your efforts.

The beginning of any endeavor is a moment filled with great power, and we are always in a state of beginning and becoming.

DECLARATION: I begin all new tasks in realistic fashion: one step at a time in the direction of my target. In this way, I can feel relaxed, calm, and confident about the whole journey.

REFLECTION: What have I been attempting to begin in my life but have been putting off because it seems overwhelming? What would be the first three steps in getting me started? What one thing can I do today to move in that direction?

Cycles

CYCLES · There is only one constant in life—change. Welcome and respect the cycles of change. Nature's cycles are inevitable, and fighting them is not a healthy option. The moon rises; the sun sets; winter turns to spring as the seasons pass. Moods shift: some days you're up, others you're down. It's hot, then it's not; you lose, then win; you're in a slump, then back in action. All things follow cyclical patterns, and all who experience success are bound to experience failure as well.

The University of Maryland women's lacrosse team won seven consecutive national championships, an amazing accomplishment by anyone's standards and a run that has not been challenged. Still, it has been eight years since their last win as of this writing. We believe this is the cyclical nature of life at work, and it can be observed in all arenas of performance.

Change is inherently good because it presents opportunities to grow, expand, and create something new. Cycles are a necessary aspect of a full, rich life. In Buddhist thought, one can never be in harmony with the universe unless one embraces its cyclical nature. Thanks to the Buddhist wisdom of both of his parents, Tiger Woods learned to embrace change and cooperate with the fluid nature of sports and life. Remember that in this life, nothing is static—and that is certain. But, we jokingly ask, is certainty static? (Hmm!)

It seems that every end is a new beginning, and the cycle perpetuates. How often do we hear about a death in a family being followed by the birth of a child? People get fired from their jobs only to experience the beginning of a new, more satisfying life. Notice and embrace your cycles of change as you dance enthusiastically with the rhythm of transformation. For our part, throughout the year, we experience the constant up-and-down, on-and-off recycling of energy in our physical disciplines, and we know that if we don't like how we feel, in time that will change and we will have renewed chi and vigor. To fight the down cycle, or to pretend you are beyond it, is to cause tension and anxiety that will exacerbate the lull. Listen to nature's way and blend with its message: change is here—enjoy it. Life is a swinging pendulum. The Buddha says: "They are wise whose thoughts are steady, unaffected by good or bad."

DECLARATION: When I am impatient with the unpleasant phase of my physical or work life cycle, I tell myself that this, too, will pass. If I resist, it will persist.

REFLECTION: What happens to me when I demonstrate resistance to the natural cycles in my physical program? What might I do differently during such times of change?

READINESS • If one is not ready, no forward movement is possible. There is an old Asian saying: "When the student is ready, the teacher appears." The truth is, the teacher was always available, but the student wasn't ready to notice.

Coaches get frustrated and impatient with their athletes who become complacent and make little effort to improve. Parents become intolerant of their children who do not seem motivated to work diligently. CEOs in major corporations wonder why certain staff are resistant to change and growth. In all of these cases, it is helpful to understand that it's not the teaching per se but rather the student who is not ready. All one can do in such a situation is to provide an environment in which others are not threatened and can grow, learn, and expand at their own natural pace—when they are, indeed, ready. In *The Art of War*, Sun Tzu mentions that a crucial rule of combat is not to count on opponents not showing up, but to instead have ways to be ready to deal with them when they do. If you are not ready, you miss the opportunity in the moment to grow, advance, and succeed. The teacher will be there when you are ready.

We suggest you leave no stone unturned in your pursuit of the extraordinary in your life. This means placing yourself in position to quickly respond to new learning, new opportunities, and new possibilities. Great warriors do this well. If you are a coach, rather than assuming blame for an athlete's complacency and lack of improvement, know that the obstacle may be as simple as a lack of readiness. Through kindness, respect, and patience, you can accelerate the process of becoming ready. Give the complacent athlete much love.

DECLARATION: I do all I can to place myself in position to strike and get what I like. I am ready, eager, and able to advance in this life.

REFLECTION: What are some examples from my past when I wasn't ready to go forward, and how could I have changed that for better results? What one thing can I do today to position myself to be readier tomorrow for personal advancement in sports, fitness, and life?

Chi

CHI • The Chinese symbol for *chi* (also spelled qi) depicts a direct connection to the divine force of life, with the very first calligraphic brushstroke pulling this force down into our inner being. Then, the three horizontal strokes represent the immediate opening to the sky, the world around us, and the earth below, where we become nourished and grow. Finally, with a sweeping upward stroke, we combine all three dimensions of this force with one swoop; and from the center (our dantien, or belly) we reach out to all eight directions to gather chi into the center of our being. As we learn to dance through the rapidly moving strokes of this magical symbol, we will become completely energized—all chi'ed up.

In Chinese, chi (ki in Japanese) is that deep, dynamic spiritual life force or energy experienced when mind and body are in sync. Chi is everywhere at all times; it is ever present. Sky, earth, oceans, rivers, forests, mountains, and streams all have chi. There is environmental chi, both clear and polluted. There are pleasant chi and annoying chi. It is everywhere you look and in everything you feel. It is within each of us; it is our breath of life. It is inner strength or weakness, impossible to see and difficult to explain, yet easy to experience. All physical activity stimulates its flow: running, yoga, dance, Tai Chi, and more. The breath-watching meditation technique we teach in this book restores chi.

Through visualization, you can project this spiritual energy into any arena of performance prior to engaging in it. For example, before an event, visualize and feel yourself moving with full spirit and energy, your adrenaline flowing freely. Feel the joy and exhilaration as you move effortlessly to your own rhythm and inner dance. Feel the transition from standing around to participating. Notice how easy it is to access your chi.

There are ten specific things you can do that will create positive, high-level chi in your life. Practice having thoughts that are positive; meditate on a daily basis; create a consciousness about healthy food; reduce or eliminate low-energy substances in your diet like alcohol, caffeine, and drugs; list seven things that you appreciate in your life (health, friends, mental acuity, home, education, etc.) and go about your day with these in mind; listen to music that uplifts your spirit; make a collage of inspirational photos and keep them where you can see them every day; choose to spend your time with highly functional, energetic people; get outside and into nature each day; and perform a random act of kindness daily. With practice and positive mental focus, you can experience this inner chi power consistently.

DECLARATION: I am aware of my sacred power of chi and practice using it prior to beginning all physical activity. Breathing and visualization help restore this inner power.

REFLECTION: What are some of the ways in which I can employ this special energy, not only in sports and fitness, but in other aspects of daily life? What can I do now to access this chi?

Effortlessness

EFFORTLESSNESS • According to the *I Ching*, there is wisdom in using four ounces to deflect four thousand pounds. In *The Art of War*, Sun Tzu strongly recommends that we follow the way of least effort. In Chinese, this effortless way of being is called wu wei, meaning "do not force the doing that is not natural." All the secrets of success in the Asian martial arts are based on this philosophy of wu wei. To push, force, or fight the flow is to cause tension and tightness; it is not natural.

Observe fish in turbulent water. They overcome this obstacle by effortlessly surfing on the swirling eddies, by going with the flow. In the same way, you may want to follow nature's law, blend with the force, and make the effort to exert less effort.

Martial artists have known for centuries that less effort makes you more proficient and spiritually sane. In the sport of running, too much effort blocks your chi and diminishes your power. Olympians have discovered that giving 90 percent effort not only is more relaxing but can also result in greater speed. This was easily demonstrated by Ray Norton, Tommie Smith, John Carlos, and Lee Evans back in the 1960s at San Jose State. Their coach at the time, Bud Winter, noticed they were exerting too much effort in order to run faster; this blocked their chi and diminished their power. At nine-tenths effort, they relaxed and produced faster times on the track.

The same principle applies to running uphill. The more effort you exert, the more difficult it becomes. When you lift weights, relax the muscles while keeping them firm, and notice an increase in strength. When working on a letter, a book, or an article, relax, breathe, and get into the flow by focusing on the joy and fun of writing—instantly, words will begin to appear where there were none before. You will experience an inner peace and strength when you choose to practice wu wei, the effortless effort, action without force.

DECLARATION: Wu wei all the way! I notice how I gain more by doing less. I love the effortless effort.

REFLECTION: As I review what I need to accomplish in my daily life, how can I do what needs to be done more effortlessly? How can I begin to apply the 90 percent law to my sport and fitness?

FATIGUE • Fatigue is always a factor in sports, fitness, and other kinds of performance. To resist it means fighting the inevitable visit by this unwelcome friend, and the anxiety and tension you create in the fight cause even greater fatigue. To triumph over fatigue, assume a yielding posture by refusing to force it away or become angry at it. Essentially, it helps to know that fatigue is a natural response brought on by overexertion. It's the body's way of telling you to eat, rest, or reevaluate your training program.

Acknowledging this universal truth, the warrior can relax, thereby relieving some of the fatigue. Say to it: "Hi, fatigue ... I'm busy right now. Thank you and good-bye." Refuse to give more power to this nuisance as you return your focus to the task at hand. Perhaps you can focus on small, manageable segments, or on how close you are to the finish line, or on your mechanics, form, pace, and other important little things.

Talk yourself through the fatigue by reminding yourself that everybody experiences it at this point in the activity or event. It's the price we all pay for breaking through our limitations. You can chant, sing, or affirm to yourself: "I feel strong— I can do it." Tell your body that you will give it sufficient rest when the activity is complete.

In many situations, you might well remember that fatigue is a feeling all warriors experience prior to entering the next level of their potential. Such a positive attitude can reduce the pain to a tolerable level. Nonresistance, yielding, and blending with fatigue will help reduce it as you discover a new-found energy.

Whatever technique you use, remember: fatigue is a natural force that is an inherent aspect of exertion. It will always be a factor. If you blend and flow with it, it will fade into the background.

DECLARATION: Don't resist and it won't persist. Fatigue is a familiar friend, a necessary entity in exploring my potential.

REFLECTION: What have I learned from my past experiences with fatigue? What do I plan to do when fatigue strikes again?

Practice

PRACTICE • According to Sun Tzu in *The Art of War*, the war is won before the battle begins. Years of experience have convinced us that tomorrow's competitive event is won in today's practice, before the war ever begins. The *I Ching* reminds us that attention to detail through consistent, intentional practice positions us for extraordinary performance.

In Buddhist teaching, practice is the way of mastery. It's the eagerness to do everything necessary to be the absolute best you can be. The warrior journey of mastery may be a thousand miles, but it begins with a single, high-quality first step called diligent preparation. This focus on the initial step alone is considered success.

The Chinese symbol for practice shows a young bird flapping its wings continually until it learns to fly. Remember this metaphor when you wish to "fly" in any arena of performance. Like this aviator, you must repeat, over and over, the practice of a certain skill until your spirit takes flight, soaring to enormous heights.

We encourage our network of performers to practice each day as if they are preparing for an important recital or a national championship game; in other words, such preparation is usually done with greater-than-usual focus, intention, and intensity. We invite them to prepare as if this were their last chance to prove their worth as performers. When they make this level of commitment, their performance is extraordinary. The great champions—Jordan, Woods, Armstrong, Gretsky, and Brady—demonstrate the courage to prepare consistently in practice with game-time intensity.

You don't become a champion; you choose to *be* one now, in practice. Cyclists know that self-mastery means time in the saddle, mile after mile. Trust that consistent, intentional preparation is, in itself, extraordinary behavior.

DECLARATION: Practicing through diligent, consistent preparation is the joy and achievement I experience. Mastery is the practice itself. Results are the by-product of my efforts in preparing for extraordinary performances.

REFLECTION: What three things have I not been doing that I can do in today's practice to help me kick my performance up a notch or two?

INJURY • We ask that you observe nature and understand and appreciate both the cycles of increase and the cycles of deterioration. For most athletes, physical injury is an inevitable recurrence of decrease. It is nature's way of telling you that something is not right. You must not resist it. Think wu wei and yield to the injury. It is reality. The sooner you can accept this, the sooner healing can take place. Begin to affirm the following in order to stay on track: "Every day in every way, I get healthier and healthier. I am strong and vibrant." These words will point you in the direction of positive attitudes toward recovery.

Taking this approach doesn't alter the fact that when serious injury appears, it turns your world upside down. You will experience panic, tension, fear, anger, frustration, depression, or a combination of these during the various stages of recovery. Such emotional turmoil creates more stress, which exacerbates the existing pain. To cope psychologically, focus on the positive aspects of your life, those things you appreciate most. We suggest you reread the discussion on gratitude in Part I.

Use this period of recovery as a time for not only recuperation but for reflection as well. Reflect upon your life: What is going well? What needs work? Reevaluate your training program and priorities and put your life into perspective. Reconnect with others who have experienced loss through injury. This will help you gain hope and confidence while reducing the fear and other churning emotions you may be experiencing.

Injury is a crisis for the injured and for those who care about them. In Chinese, the word for *crisis* includes both danger and opportunity: opportunity blowing on a dangerous wind. We encourage you to search for hidden opportunities during this difficult period.

The *I Ching* tells us: "Nurture your mind and body ... look for wisdom in your acceptance of the times." Be sure to meditate and then visualize your injury healing itself. This will reduce anxiety, subdue pain, and hasten recovery. After meditating and quieting the mind, feel your injured area becoming more and more relaxed. Imagine how it feels as the pain subsides. See the area going from a deep red to a lighter shade of pink—pink being the color of healthy tissue. Feel yourself performing once again, pain free.

DECLARATION: My injury is an opportunity for me to learn what I need to know and do in my athletic and personal life. Every day, in every way, I get healthier and stronger.

REFLECTION: What has my past or present injury taught me about my sport, fitness, or life? What steps can I take to diminish the risk of injury and illness?

PAUSE • The Chinese symbol for pause depicts a person in a small roadside pavilion taking some time to view the scenery and enjoy a few moments of self-reflection. When recharged and rested, he continues the journey.

In today's world, it seems as though more is better when, in reality, less is actually more. Still, when you think about taking down time and resting for a few days, you may fear you will fall behind, lose your edge, and sacrifice the advantage to your competitor—who, like the Energizer Bunny, never stops working. Jerry remembers a time when he would train twice a day, seven days a week doing mega-mileage workouts until one day the bottom fell out and he self-destructed. Injury, burnout, chronic fatigue, and lackluster performance plagued him for quite a while. Then a musician friend reminded him that less is more: "Truly great music is the result of the pause or space between the notes. Musical pauses are not a lack of action; they are an integral part of the action." His was a true warrior mentality.

So it is with your workout regimen. Regardless of your sport or activity, getting in great physical or mental shape requires rest (pause), space between workouts and events. We must realize that our cellular structure is fragile and must have periods of rest. It amounts to the age-old battle between moderation and excessiveness. Excessiveness is a cancer of the soul. It forces you to lose motivation and joy. The cure for this ailment is moderation, where less becomes more. Days off from your workouts or events are a good start. Do fewer reps with weights, take shorter runs, work fewer hours, and enjoy the pause for what it truly is … a refreshing time-out. Moderation helps restore balance, increases excitement and enthusiasm, and restores the motivation to continue something you love to do. The moderate warrior knows how to "fondle" the body and mind into shape as opposed to excessively forcing or pushing it there. "Fondle, don't force" is a useful mantra in this regard.

Concerning the value of rest, Buddhist thought invites you to seek moderation in all things. "Even in moderation?" we ask.

DECLARATION: When in doubt, cut it out; rest is best. I seek opportunities to rest and give my mind and body a chance to regenerate and get stronger.

REFLECTION: What is my worst fear about taking a rest or pause in my workouts or work? What positive effects could I experience from a well-timed pause? How can I initiate a pause in my routine now?

Slumps

SLUMPS • The cycles of life cannot be hastened. Slumps are natural physical, mental, emotional, and spiritual cycles. They are inevitable occurrences in all arenas of performance. There are two kinds of performers: those who go into a slump and those who will go into one. Slumps are the common ground that unites all who pursue the physical, athletic life. That said, you must refuse to fight them, choosing instead to focus on the little things, the process rather than outcomes or results. In this way, you can relax and build confidence. When you fight slumps, you create more pressure, tension, and anxiety, thereby exacerbating an already dismal situation.

Slumps are the natural lowest points of the perpetual pendulum swing in life's ups and downs. Only when you fully surrender to the downswing at the very bottom can you begin to experience the natural, exhilarating, and effortless upswing in the growth cycle of life. You must yield to the downswing in order to perform optimally.

An effective way to yield to a slump is to focus your attention on the little things you can control and to refuse to get caught up in results—those things you cannot control. When you focus on outcomes, you get tight, tense, and tentative because they are beyond your reach. Instead, align your focus on all the essential little things that cause you to perform well.

Let's say you find that your game is off. What five essentials can you perform that, if executed well and with intent, would enable you to play well? In basketball, simply box out, crash the boards, sprint your lanes, or dive for the 50/50 ball. If you are speaking before a large audience, make eye contact, project your voice, vary your tone, be sincere, and use inflection where it matters most. When running a race, watch your breathing, stride well, carry your arms appropriately, and focus on being fluid and relaxed. All these actions are things over which you have complete control, and they will help you relax, stay calm, and become more confident.

Slumps happen when you try to force results instead of simply doing all the things that allow you to perform naturally. Remember that the strong, flexible branches of the bamboo tree yield to the wind and survive. The rigid pine tree cracks and falls. Resisting slumps is counterproductive. Meditation and visualization exercises can help you recapture your natural rhythm as you *feel* the performance you wish to regain. While visualizing, affirm to yourself, "Soft is strong." Paradoxically enough, when you give up trying to control your downswings and slumps, you gain control and begin to fly.

DECLARATION: Slumps are natural cycles. When I enter one, I choose to focus on the little things and watch the big things happen. When I let go of outcomes and results, I regain my natural rhythm.

REFLECTION: When I am performing at my best at what I do, what contributes to this? How can I bring this to my game and life during a slump?

PLATEAU • From the very beginning of your journey on the road of physical training, you will occasionally encounter periods during which you make no progress and become frustrated and disgruntled. What you may fail to realize at such times is that you are experiencing what everyone else experiences as well: the sacred space called plateau.

Plateaus in sports, fitness, family life, and business are a natural part of the process of achieving. In fact, we want you to know that most worthwhile learning happens during these periods of plateau. For this reason alone, love and embrace this delightful stage of improvement. We ask that you accept this time as natural and essential: a time when body and mind catch up to your new, emerging level of performance. It provides opportunities for deeper learning and self-mastery. This is the sacred purpose of the plateau, and most of us fail to realize its importance.

So many athletes, fitness buffs, parents, and business professionals become frustrated and fight times of plateau, feeling that they are stagnating and not improving. This is both incorrect and counterproductive. Listen to ancient warrior wisdom and accept this plateau stage as nature's way of perfecting what you have recently learned. In Chinese, a plateau is actually the mountaintop, built upon the ground base of Earth. It is the Earth elevating itself from this base. This mountaintop is where you now are—that secure, grounded place that is already at the top. You are here for a period of time, and one day you will wake up and think that you've reached a higher level overnight when, in reality, you've been slowly developing during this grounded, learning plateau phase.

DECLARATION: I accept my plateaus as important stages of development during which my body is adjusting to new levels of excellence never reached before. Without plateau, I will not go—ahead.

REFLECTION: If I could embrace my plateaus in this way, what effect would this have on my physical, emotional, and spiritual life? What obstacles to shifting to this way of thinking stand in my way?

Part IV: Transformation
From Sole to Soul

You have arrived at the fourth and final stage of your journey: one of transformation and change, the stage of allowing your body to nourish your soul. As you begin to age in life, you may notice that you have accumulated a wonderful base of experience and wisdom, giving you a splendid opportunity to transform yourself. Such change is nature's way of fostering continual growth. When spring comes, grass grows and caterpillars morph into butterflies. You must learn to acknowledge and accept this natural force and surrender to it in your personal, emotional, and physical life. But change requires extraordinary courage, suffering, and trust because it demands that you go outside your comfort zone—mentally, physically, and spiritually—and become comfortable with being uncomfortable.

Try standing up and raising your arms above your head as if to touch the ceiling. Hold them there. Now, reach up a few more inches and hold them again. Feel the stretch becoming uncomfortable. Hold it, hold it ... now, stretch two more inches and continue to hold until it gets very uncomfortable. This is the feeling of discomfort you may have to experience in order to go outside your comfort zone. You must go beyond what you've known, who you are, and how you perceive yourself. Yet here is where the exciting challenge is, where growth takes place if you are willing to take a leap of faith. Here is a splendid opportunity to transform yourself. This demands being in that sacred, uncomfortable space where competitors become partners, loss is gain, soft is strong, and less is more. This is the soul work of the warrior, where one goes from sole to soul, from sport to spirituality. But if you are to fly, you must take the leap and trust it will all work out.

We can illustrate this point with the following story. One early Sunday morning, Jerry went running with a Catholic nun high in the Sierra Madre Mountains of eastern California. After beginning with an intense, strenuous, demanding climb on rocky trails, they arrived at a brilliantly lit meadow at 9,500 feet. A huge herd of mule deer was playing in the pasture while two red-tailed hawks glided on a downdraft, searching for breakfast. Deep blue Lake Tahoe sparkled in the distance. As they paused to imbibe nature's beauty, Sister Marion quietly whispered, as if in a church, "Jerry, I feel closer to my maker at this moment than I do in any other part of my life." She put into words in that instant what Jerry had experienced and known for years yet had never felt free to express. Thanks to this insightful nun, he now had certified permission to affirm and assert more candidly this spiritual, sacred, godlike, soulful connection to his athletic and fitness life. Now, each day he eagerly awaits his chance to run and bike on mountainous, single-track trails in nature's house of worship. As a result, he feels the positive effects of this sole-to-soul connection, and his overall performance and well-being thrive in extraordinary ways.

Taking this concept of sole to soul to another level are the Zen Buddhist priests living high in the mountains of Japan who seek awareness, enlightenment, and wisdom by subjecting themselves to extraordinary pain and suffering, running extreme distances of twenty-five to fifty-plus miles every day for several consecutive months. These marathon monks experience through their regimented physical rituals a kind of practical spiritual education for personal growth and development. Properly guided, this sacred, strenuous physical regimen becomes their microcosmic classroom, an inroad into their deeper selves, an honorable and worthy journey from sole to soul.

Although you may not follow in the footsteps of these monks, you can transform your relationship with your personal and physical life. Notice that when you are in this sacred space in your physical routines, you act with integrity: you do the workouts and the training; you narrow the gap between what you say and what you do. You are courageous and committed. You recognize the inherent value of teammates and opponents and demonstrate respect for sport itself. You admire the dedication to the little things accomplished with brilliance rather than the brilliant things done in marginal fashion. You are open, receptive, trusting, vulnerable, and confident, and you are aware that you are part of a larger game, greater than any you play. We think you'll appreciate this world of transformation. Please enter.

INTEGRITY

Hold to your ethics and principles and do not compromise what you believe to be right. Acting with integrity is the key.

I Ching 29

How far you go in athletics, fitness, and life is directly influenced by the scope of your integrity. The Chinese symbols for integrity illustrate wholeness of character and a commitment to stand up for personal principles—never for a moment considering compromising what you believe to be right. Buddhist thought asks that you do the right thing, act with integrity in all things. For us, integrity is the act of narrowing the existential gap between what you say or feel and what you do.

Physical activity presents you with continual opportunities to demonstrate your integrity. You may say you train hard, yet when others are not looking, you back off the intensity. You may say you'll show up but don't. You might claim you want to get in shape, yet indulge in counterproductive eating habits. There are many ways this gap between what you say and do can manifest.

There is another way you can compromise your integrity that happens frequently in sports: not playing to your full potential. Integrity is the refusal to compromise your talents regardless of the score, the outcome, or the differences in levels of ability among competitors. Do not give others permission to make you feel inferior, undeserving, or less than you are.

For extraordinary athletes like Tiger Woods and quarterback Tom Brady, integrity of effort seems to matter more than winning or losing. Some talented athletes, however, play down against an inferior opponent or give up against a superior foe. In doing so, they compromise their integrity. Warriors go to battle and refuse to let up, play down, or run away from losing by playing tentatively or cautiously against an opponent. You show a lack of integrity when you back down out of fear or intimidation or when you give others permission to make you feel inferior or unworthy. This journey asks that you demonstrate integrity every chance you get and feel the power of being a true winner.

DECLARATION: I consistently look for openings where I can narrow the gap between who I am, what I say, and what I do.

REFLECTION: How do I demonstrate a lack of integrity in my workouts? What are some concrete things I can do to create more integrity in my life? What effect would this have on my performance?

MASTERY • It is interesting to discover that there is no path to mastery: mastery is the path, the journey of never-ending multidimensional growth and development, a zigzag way of excellence. You don't attain mastery; you live it as a lifestyle one small step at a time, and you can measure success by the quality of those steps.

It is the process of engaging in your physical activity itself and how you go about it that indicate mastery. When you try to understand mastery from a Chinese perspective, you learn that it is not hierarchical in nature. To be a master is to be a person who has simply (but easily) mastered the art of living in all endeavors. A master is a perpetual student, always learning self-cultivation. A master never considers himself to be on top or numero uno. A master never gets tired of learning. Masters always experiment with and embrace new challenges and dive into ever more enigmatic and intricate problems on their path toward solving the mysteries of living.

As we mentioned earlier, most athletes and performers become impatient and frustrated with the periods of time they spend at a plateau. They think they are stagnating and floundering. Many are intolerant of their seeming lack of improvement. In his book *The Way of Aikido*, martial artist George Leonard defines mastery as that "mysterious process through which what is first difficult becomes easy through diligent, patient, long-term practice." Know that practice is, according to most expert opinion, more important than talent when it comes to masterful, extraordinary performance. You simply need to trust this notion as part of the overall Spirit of the Dancing Warrior journey. By trusting, you are already extraordinary.

Think of mastery as a river: it flows forward only to suddenly change direction and appear to reverse itself back toward its beginning. The flow quickens through the narrows yet slows when it widens. The water is clean and clear yet becomes murky and cloudy. You cannot fight the change or push the river. Mastery is giving yourself over to the river and trusting that all things happen for a reason. This is true progress on the warrior path in athletics, fitness, and life.

DECLARATION: Mastery is a process, not a destination. I live the way of mastery each day as a lifestyle of diligent practice and preparation.

REFLECTION: What do I need to start doing that I'm not doing in order to enter the realm of mastery in sports, fitness, and work? What obstacles stand in my way, keeping me from executing these items?

SUFFERING · The physical life is difficult; it can be excruciatingly uncomfortable, physically, emotionally, and spiritually. But we know that if you wish to improve, you need to suffer or become uncomfortable. By their very nature, sports and fitness, while they bring joy and satisfaction, evoke suffering in all of us: we sometimes have feelings of frustration, fear, grief, sadness, regret, anger, anxiety, or despair. This is exactly like life as a whole but more intense and occurring over a shorter duration.

Jerry has worked extensively and intimately with young men and women athletes at the collegiate level, and he is always awed by the complete range of emotions they can experience in a single forty- or sixty-minute contest. For most students on campus, it may take three or four months to experience what an athlete will experience emotionally, mentally, spiritually, and socially during one athletic event. Whenever you seek advancement and higher levels of performance in any aspect of life, you experience some element of suffering. But when you leave your comfort zone and become uncomfortable, notice how expansive your potential truly is.

Buddhist thought tells us that we must accept suffering as a way of life; this is the first of Four Noble Truths in Zen. All greatness, awareness, and acute sensitivity are the natural outcomes of adversity and suffering. There is a wonderful story of an elite university athlete who was at death's door due to a serious ailment. Following nine months in the hospital, he recovered, and within a year he returned to his team. His awareness, appreciation, and sensitivity enabled him to work extra hard on the field and do more than was asked of him because he was enormously grateful to be alive. His suffering had made him a better athlete, teammate, and person while others on the team still cut corners, only working hard when the coaches were present. The lessons he learned from his suffering changed his entire outlook on life. Now he is called "the team Buddha."

The warrior knows that in suffering—experiencing painful feelings or being uncomfortable—you begin to see the more meaningful side of athletics and fitness and life. There is wisdom in the existential experience of suffering. Deep appreciation is often the residual benefit. When you can take this stance, you grow, learn, blossom, and connect with your warrior within. Lance Armstrong, seven-time winner of the Tour de France, tells us that he embraced suffering and welcomed its challenges.

DECLARATION: I welcome my physical journey with all its suffering and pain, and as a result, I reach the far boundaries of my full human potential.

REFLECTION: With regard to my physical life, what kinds of suffering and sacrifice could contribute to my overall improvement and growth? What stops me from embracing the suffering?

Courage

COURAGE • Courage describes those who are willing to take calculated risks and have frequent encounters with danger. Such behavior makes us inwardly strong, instilling a profound awareness of life filled with new meaning and richness. Risk taking requires courage, which comes from the French word *coeur*: heart. This kind of heart requires innate strength; it cannot rely on blind pride, simply daring to take a leap.

We certainly encourage taking calculated risks that have the potential to lead to significant breakthroughs in your sport or other activities in life. A perfect example of this is in progress in Jerry's life as of this writing. He and his family are relocating to Boulder, Colorado, from their home in Santa Cruz, California. They are all hoping this shift will create opportunities to enhance an already good life. But there is a huge amount of stress involved, and they could eventually decide to return to California. But by calculating the worst-case scenarios, they came to the conclusion that the risks and stress will be worth the effort, that there is the potential to discover a better way of life.

Visionary author Ray Bradbury, one of America's greatest creative geniuses, has offered scintillating advice about risk taking: "First you jump off the cliff and you build your wings on the way down and fly." Like the warrior, however, you must develop a high tolerance for failure when you jump, understanding that all setbacks are ways to learn how to enhance performance. Failure is your essential and inevitable teacher. For every step back, you go forward two.

Courage demands that you be fearless like the hermit crab, who leaves his protective home and risks being exposed to predators as he searches for a bigger and better shell. Like the courageous crab, you must learn to be comfortable with being uncomfortable if you are to experience the extraordinary. Remember, the crab risks his life—you don't. Philosopher André Gide said you "cannot discover new oceans unless you have the courage to lose sight of the shore."

In Chinese, the word for *courage* also implies daring to go beyond one's limits. Dare to lose by trying because not trying is the more painful loss.

DECLARATION: I am a courageous, risk-taking warrior who possesses a high tolerance for setbacks. Risks are the dues I pay for breakthroughs.

REFLECTION: What risks could I take that would improve my performance? My life? What is the worst-case scenario if I take the risk and it doesn't work out?

TRUST • The Chinese symbols for trust evoke an inner sense of trust in others and ourselves and the courage to believe in the natural evolution of things. In sports and other physical activities, circumstances sometimes unfold in a way that is contrary to how you think they should. During such disappointing times, trust in the process is crucial. When you do, you ward off tension, stress, and pressure and ultimately experience success. Every one of the thirty-plus national championship teams Jerry has had the honor of working with has exhibited extensive trust in athletes and staff. Everyone had each other's back. They did what they agreed to do, worked hard for each other, and never doubted that everyone was on board with the purpose of the season. Their intentions were aligned, and their actions suggested the direction they were headed. Trust that life flows, like a river, in all directions yet continues steadily toward its destination. Everything is exactly as it is supposed to be.

Nature consistently sends messages to us that point the way, signs that help us stay on the right path in following our dreams. Your progress may be slower than you desire, but like the warrior, see the wisdom in the plateau and trust nature's way. When you plant flowers, you do not pull them up to force them to grow faster or taller; you trust nature's way and let them progress naturally. It is no different on the warrior path of extraordinary performance. Life's unfolding of events is as apparent as the coming and going of the seasons; all is exactly as it must be. Trust your instincts, trust your talents and gifts, trust the process, and let things take their natural course. To win a national championship, run a successful business, or raise a healthy family, it is essential to have trust in yourself and those around you.

DECLARATION: As my life unfolds before me, I trust that all things happen the way they are supposed to, not the way I think they should. I trust the flow like H_2O.

REFLECTION: How do I show my lack of trust in the process of my physical endeavors? In what specific ways can I begin to trust in it—and myself? What thoughts do I need to change in order to demonstrate self-trust?

YIN YANG · In our Western world of sports and fitness, we are trained to be dualistic, comfortable with distinction: either in shape or not; either a winner or a loser; too fast or too slow; soft or strong; flexible or inflexible. But in Chinese thought there is no split between yin and yang, as they are balanced opposites and integrated into one undivided whole. All dualistic opposites are actually *one*. Night and day are actually one whole twenty-four-hour cycle; less is actually more; soft is also strong; going slower could propel you faster; not doing is doing; opponents are partners. Neutralizing dualities helps you develop strength and allow higher levels of performance to be possible.

If you are too yang, you are unnecessarily aggressive and too outcome oriented and as a result will become tight, nervous, and tense. This leads to mistakes and setbacks. If you are too yin, you are too passive and self-conscious, causing you to be timid and unassertive; you become too hesitant and tentative to achieve your potential. A cyclist can be too yang when she constantly attacks the hills in a race rather than assessing the right moment to challenge her opponent. A basketball team can be too yin if they play it safe. By balancing yin and yang, the warrior stays in harmony with the flow, with the natural way of sports. You need to develop the right timing and let the game come to you. You can be both passive and aggressive as you lull your opponents to sleep—you can be easygoing, then attack with the ferocity of a tiger. Soft is strong as you relax and become more powerful. Use these opposites to great advantage when you do push-ups or lift weights. Keep your arms firm (yang) to support the body, yet soften the muscles (yin), and notice how much easier it is to complete a set of fifteen. We encourage you to blend with this paradoxical mystery of yin-yang opposites and mix both for extraordinary performance.

DECLARATION: I look for ways to neutralize opposites by seeing how each extreme is, indeed, an important part of the whole. Less is often more.

REFLECTION: When is less more; when is soft strong? When does the mind dance? When does the body think? How does understanding these paradoxes help my performance?

Egolessness

EGOLESSNESS • All arenas of performance provide you with the opportunity to learn to rise above the hindrance of egocentricity. In Zen practice, you learn how greatness and self-mastery are achieved through egoless detachment from oneself. Egocentricity is a hindrance to performance. The athlete or performer who needs to boast and impress others is usually doing so out of feelings of deep insecurity and uncertainty. He therefore depletes the chi so necessary for firm, strong action. Champions appear reserved and without ego, almost as if they are too nice to compete, almost too weak to be a threat. Yet when the game is on the line, they fight to the death in ego-less fashion. It seems as though egolessness is always rewarded, whether in athletics or in other aspects of life.

The warrior realizes how consistent ego involvement creates interference with one's performance. Much chi is wasted in your effort to defend your greatness. In an ironic twist, your ego gets what it desires by stroking the egos of others. We want to encourage you to look for opportunities to sincerely celebrate and affirm the journey of friends and competitors, nurturing them on their path to personal greatness. Let them know how much you appreciate their high level of play and how enjoyable it was to experience their greatness. After all, the better they compete, the better you become. Notice how such action helps you as well.

As a warrior, know that any ego-related behavior creates unnecessary anxiety and tension due to the relentless need to live up to your self-centered illusions. Know that less focus on self means more positive regard from others. Be humble by giving credit to others. Remember this quote from the *Tao Te Ching*: "They do not make claims, therefore they are credited; they do not boast, therefore they advance."

DECLARATION: The less I talk about me, the more others will see. I take time to affirm the greatness in others.

REFLECTION: What is my real purpose in telling others about my accomplishments? What do I like least about myself and what can be done to change that? What are some things I can do to bring out the best in others?

Selflessness

SELFLESSNESS • Remember the example used earlier, that a flock of geese works together, conserving energy and flying farther by combining their efforts as they fly in a V formation instead of selfishly flying on their own. This is the power of giving and caring, which, for most of us, is counterintuitive. Taoists call this power *tz'u*, which in Chinese means "caring or compassion."

In sports, fitness, and life, we intuitively search to get, not give. You ask yourself, "What can I get from being a member of this team?" or "What can I get out of working as a coach?" Selflessness encourages you to be a servant. In fact, in Japanese the word *samurai* means "servant," the servant warrior whose purpose is to help others along the path. We have noticed that evolved individuals put themselves last, yet they are first. Giving to your teammates enhances your own performance as they look for ways to reciprocate. Look for opportunities to bring out another's best; give praise and credit to a job well done. After a beautiful bounce pass leading to a basket, the scorer running back down the court will point his index finger at his teammate who made the assist in recognition of his fine play.

Selflessness, you will observe, ultimately brings personal fulfillment and conserves energy, allowing for higher levels of play. In your sport, fitness regimen, or other activities, find ways to compliment others on how they work and how well they perform. Ask them "How can I help?" when it appears they are in need. Show interest in others' passions. Give to others for the sake of giving, without expecting anything in return.

Lao Tzu encourages selflessness as a way to bring self-fulfillment.

DECLARATION: To create more joy and fulfillment for myself and others, I remind myself that when I give, I get back a hundredfold. This is nature's law of reciprocity.

REFLECTION: In what three ways can I demonstrate the power of giving in my athletics and life? What can I do today to become more selfless?

HUMILITY • It is important to remember from the outset that humility is not about undermining your personal power. On the contrary: by being humble, you become more flexible, yielding, and open to learn. In a word, you become stronger.

The two Chinese symbols that best describe humility are *qian xu*. *Qian* describes you as a completely confident person, fully aware of your place in life and in your relationship to others. *Xu* means learning to be empty in order to fill up, then to continually recycle your fullness in order to receive new information, knowledge, and wisdom once again.

The Tao reminds us that a posture of humble heart and genuine respect will bring blessings from all directions. Humility, in sports and in all other arenas of life, is all about giving: giving credit to others, because without your opponents, teammates, coaches, parents, and other supportive people, you would not be where you are.

In Buddhist teachings, giving credit to others is called right speech, the avoidance of vain talk. Notice how those who boast of achievement have little merit. The need some people have to constantly prove themselves is exceedingly harmful, tiring, and detrimental to their mental and spiritual well-being. The warrior acts as if he has received nothing. We encourage you to feel secure in promoting others. Insecure people have a dire need to promote themselves, but you are more effective and appreciated when you demonstrate humility by focusing on the greatness of others.

In competition, there is always the risk of being too self-involved, smitten with your prowess. The code of the warrior states that the more effort you expend in looking good, the further you separate yourself from your heart; excessively self-absorbed behavior creates inner battles, engendering much self-doubt. Be proud of your achievements, cherish your well-deserved recognition, celebrate your efforts, yet focus on others' accomplishments as well, giving recognition to the greatness of those around you. "Give and in so doing gain" is a mantra worth adopting.

DECLARATION: I realize that all of my accomplishments and gifts are made possible not only through my diligent work, but through the loving efforts of all the others with me along the way. My victory is their victory.

REFLECTION: In what situations in my present life can I display humility, and how would I demonstrate this virtue? What has been my biggest blunder with regard to humility, and how would I change it in the future?

SIMPLICITY • The Chinese word for *simplicity* is *p'u*, literally meaning the uncarved block of wood in its natural state of simply being wood. Taoists embrace simplicity and limit desires for superficial adornment. When you do this, you experience a kind of freedom; this is the freedom to focus, to concentrate and be absolutely harmonious and present during a performance.

In all aspects of training, the warrior follows nature's law of simplicity: less is more. Today, sports and fitness seem to have become much too complex with all their attendant technological advances: watches, heart-rate monitors, energy bars, replacement drinks, exercise machines. Clearly much is gained, yet so much is lost. Whatever happened to listening to your body for appropriate feedback? Ethiopian Abebe Bikila won an Olympic gold medal in the marathon running barefoot. No high-tech shoes or digital timepiece for him; he simply ran. Complex gadgetry can create distraction, anxiety, and tension, hindering performance.

National-class marathoner Nancy Ditz ran her fastest marathon free of a watch. At first she was hesitant to do so, but she took the risk, listened to her internal clock, and ran the race of her life. If you have seen the movie *Tin Cup*, you have seen a classic example of someone failing to keep it simple, in the scene where Rene Russo comes to receive her golf lesson from Kevin Costner wearing so many allegedly performance-enhancing contraptions that she can barely move.

The mentality and heart of the warrior focus on back to basics, where attention is directed toward in-the-moment response to present conditions. Try simple workouts, simple diet, basic nutritious food free of chemical additives, and simple clothing. Shed the extra stuff by asking, "Do I really need this?" Many are discovering the benefits of a simpler life.

The *Tao Te Ching* says, "Know what is enough; return to simplicity." Many outstanding accomplishments come in the purest, simplest moments.

DECLARATION: Simplicity is the freedom to focus on only that which is truly important. Great things happen in times of pure simplicity. Embrace nature's way: less is more.

REFLECTION: In what ways can I streamline my life at work, at home, and with my physical activity? What effect would this have on my overall performance?

Detachment

DETACHMENT • We have noticed that whether you lose or win, one thing is certain: neither is an indication of your self-worth as an athlete or a person. Both are simply gauges that measure your performance on that given day in relation to several variables that may be beyond your control.

Detachment doesn't mean not caring about outcomes and results. Winning is fun, and the quickest path to winning is attending to the little things. When the event is completed, you simply need to detach your ego (sense of self) from the results.

Remember that you are *not* the result; you are so much more. When you can think this way (and many times you can't), you experience joy and satisfaction as well as a new personal freedom.

But it is difficult to learn the wisdom of release or detachment. It almost seems counterintuitive, like so much we have explored in this book. It takes much courage to enter into this unfamiliar place of letting go of past successes and failures and refusing to let either results dictate who you are. Attachment to outcomes is an old habit, a trap that incarcerates the mind. You can still feel discouraged, disappointed, and even depressed after a tough loss, but you must get a perspective and get on with life. According to the *Tao Te Ching*, "The stronger the attachment, the greater the cost." Learning this enables you to go back into the arena as a warrior with vitality and excitement, eager to take more risks and without the fear of putting it all on the line. Such freedom allows you to dance your game completely uninhibited, the way you were meant to. Athletes who have accomplished this claim to have felt a surge of reserves they didn't know they had.

Buddhist thought tells you that too strong an attachment to results will lead you away from the cultivation of awareness and greatness. Here's a funny thought: does this mean that the Buddha is attached to detachment? Zen is simple, but not easy.

DECLARATION: When I'm detached, my performance can't be matched. The stronger the attachment, the greater the cost.

REFLECTION: What am I attached to that stands in the way of something good happening, and what can I do to help myself detach from this?

MODERATION • Wisdom, regardless of its source, suggests that we follow nature's law of moderation and not indulge in extremes of any sort. We encourage you to strive for moderation in all you do. The Tao reminds us, however, that moderation does not necessarily mean staying safe in the middle ground. It is a concept that teaches you how to work with extremes. Remember that the trouble begins when you go to one of two extremes, such as being too high or too low. Moderation is the wise choice whereby you integrate these opposites into a coherent whole, a balance between both, resulting in an ideal state of performance.

In athletics or any other physical endeavor, learn to recognize when you have had enough of either extreme. The addictive nature of sports and fitness can sometimes make it difficult to yield to common sense, to know the delicate balance between being in your best shape and running the risk of injury or sickness. Clearly, when you are training for a major personal event, you may have to go outside the line and disrupt the balance or moderation. Just remember to swing back toward the center when the event is complete.

You may observe that there is nothing better than moderation; consider this an invitation to avoid excess in aspects of life outside the athletic realm such as social activity, work, and diet. Remember that excess in any arena can usher in disorder, disaster, burnout, and fatigue. Leisure, for example, is good, yet too much of it can lead to restlessness. Work is important, yet in excess it causes havoc in other parts of life. Exercise and sports create vibrancy and wellness, but in overabundance they can strip away the vibrancy one has gained. The warrior learns to dance between the two extremes with great agility. Learn to walk the moderate way.

The Buddha teaches, "Everything in moderation." To which we reply: "Moderation is everything."

DECLARATION: Excel without excess. I realize my dreams when I avoid the extremes. Balance is power!

REFLECTION: What aspects of my training, diet, work, and life can I trim to avoid excess and as a result be better off? In any aspect of my life, in what ways am I addicted to excess?

NOW • In his classic *The Way of Zen*, Alan Watts refers to what Western mystics call the Eternal Now, the state of one-pointed awareness, this "one moment" in the sense of being focused in the present. Being parked in the present without focusing on past experiences or fears of the future is the very essence of Eastern thought. This is what makes Tiger Woods so competitively dangerous. He can, unlike so many others, play each shot one at a time as if it were the only thing that mattered.

The warrior has learned that in all physical activity he must be focused in the here and now to experience optimal performance. He knows what we all need to know, that being in the now is pure joy and satisfaction. Watts points out that you don't dance to get to some other place; you don't sing to get to the end of the song. Neither should you work out, train, run, swim, bike, or do your job just to get it done. Focus on the joy of the process—minute by minute, day by day.

To help you focus like this, direct your attention to all the wonderful things going on inside your body as you train. Feel the blood flow through the arterial pathways. Remind yourself that every moment you train and work is an investment in mental and physical health, one that pays dividends for years to come. Focus your eyes only on what you are doing: the ball, the rim, the field, the weights, the book you are writing. Choose a good visual target. Fill your ears with words of encouragement and positive expressions. Perhaps listen to music that facilitates concentration in the moment. Or think about the runner who took all the numbers and hands from the face of his watch and wrote in the word *now*. Wow! He had the correct time, every second of the day. Try to plan your life as if you were to live forever, yet act as if this is your last day on earth. Carpe diem: seize the day. In the words of Martin Luther King Jr., feel "the fierce urgency of now."

DECLARATION: What time is it? *Now*! I always perform at my best when I focus on the here and now. *Now* is *how* performance becomes *wow*!

REFLECTION: Today, when my mind starts racing toward the future and I begin to become overwhelmed with chores and work to do, I will ask myself this question: "What can I do today, since that is all I have?"

Epilogue: Completion
From Tao to How

Even though it seems impossible to define the ineffable Tao in Western terms, the concept has become universally accepted as the Way of natural truth; it encourages you to notice nature at work and then act and flow with it accordingly. In a nutshell, Tao means *how*—how things work. For the purposes of Spirit of the Dancing Warrior's, notice how the warrior journey works; it is a circular process as opposed to a linear one: from here to there, a start and a finish, and completion with emphasis on outcomes and results. The warrior's path is akin to the universal symbol of the open circle that has no beginning or end yet is already an ever-expanding whole. The circle is never closed, symbolizing the unlimited creative power within the individual. The essence of the warrior path is not its product but its process. Within this process, the warrior understands human nature with all its complexities so well that he or she uses the least amount of energy and resistance along the way.

In this section, called "Completion," we wish to emphasize that this journey and this book are complete but do not end.

They renew themselves in cyclical fashion, moving in a consistent, steady manner, always returning to the source amid the peaks and ebbs of each day, week, month, or year. You will notice how your energy fluctuates naturally when you play, train, and compete, all the while learning to live more creatively, more wisely, more productively, and with greater inspiration when you align with the Tao of your heart.

Notice the Tao of the warrior, or *how* the journey works. For example, Warriorship means spontaneity: *tze jan*. This enables you to look within and become one with your natural self as you learn to instinctively transcend your separateness and unify your body, mind, heart, and soul.

The warrior also demonstrates cooperative action with nature's way, the principle of harmonious behavior: wu wei. You work with the wind as you draft behind a teammate on a bike; you do not try to conquer the mountain as a skier, instead blending with its contours and undulations. When you learn to cooperate with *how* things are, you begin to experience fluidity and flexibility within your physical, emotional, and spiritual life.

When you become conscious of and learn to balance polar opposites, yin and yang, you learn *how* to become aligned and in harmony with the Tao of the warrior. You develop the ability to think outside the box and accept such dualities as slow and fast, victory and defeat, soft and strong, less and more without distinction, as these seeming opposites are actually part of the greater whole. By so doing, you develop greater awareness, strength, and satisfaction and elevated levels of performance in athletics, fitness, and life.

When you develop the warrior trait *te*, you begin to learn *how* to fulfill your greatest potential. With te, the warrior sees setbacks and failure as opportunities to learn; stays in the moment and puts aside outcomes and results; ceases to be self-critical and accepts the true natural self; exhibits courage and integrity at the risk of being different; and takes action with enthusiasm while not being overly concerned about what happens. This, at its best, is the essence of *how* personal power is expressed—warrior power.

Profoundly, the Spirit of the Dancing Warrior's journey is a Tao, a way. It is truly a sacred spiritual training that teaches you the verities of life and invaluable lessons about commitment, courage, conscientiousness, fear, failure, success, patience, persistence, perseverance, confidence, passion, dedication, and many other essential ingredients so necessary for personal growth and inner expansion. This rich, precious time with sports and other physical activities prepares you to respond to the everyday microdrama of life, its ups and downs, joys and sadness, successes and setbacks.

When you observe the world at large, you probably notice that so many of us seem to avoid the positive opportunities for self-development that sports and fitness provide on a daily basis. Many ships are in the water, but a relative few go out to sea; even fewer have the courage to lose sight of the shore, and if they do, they often fail to persevere, giving up just prior to the lighthouse appearing on the horizon. *Spirit of the Dancing Warrior* gives you the opportunity to go inside yourself, dig deep, and discover the courage to realize your fullest physical, emotional, and spiritual potential, and to take this gift and apply it to the search for the extraordinary in all you do.

The wise and enlightened always know that from little streams come big rivers. On this warrior journey from ordinary to extraordinary, we remind you of the importance of focusing on the little things, the small details involved in this process of athletic activity, and let the big results come as a natural by-product. Remember this: you are always extraordinary when you execute the little things brilliantly and leave the marginal execution of the brilliant things to those who choose to be ordinary.

Choose this as your work and commit yourself to it with all your heart. When you commit, you will experience profound wisdom and inspiration for and about all of life. While reflecting on his own athletic path in his book *The Hero's Journey*, scholar and mythologist Joseph Campbell recalls the period of his life when he was a world-class athlete while at Columbia University: "That was a beautiful, beautiful period. I think that meant more to me than anything else, my running on the track. I learned more about living from that time than any other time in my life."

It is our hope and desire that on this hero's journey of the Spirit of the Dancing Warrior you will learn much about yourself, your sport, and your life. Let *Spirit of the Dancing Warrior* guide and comfort you along the path, whether in victory or defeat, whether you're up or down, happy or sad. It is all part of learning, growing, and coming into your own on this physio-spiritual journey from ordinary to extraordinary.

Jerry Lynch

Jerry Lynch, PhD is an internationally and nationally recognized sports psychologist, life coach, speaker, and national-class athlete. Over the past twenty-five years, he has worked with professional teams, athletes, and coaches in the NBA, NFL, NLL, and PGA as well as thirty-three national championship teams and athletes at universities such as Maryland, Duke, Stanford, North Carolina, Oregon State, Columbia, Colorado, Ohio State, Arkansas, Missouri, and UC Santa Cruz. He is the author of ten books and the father of four athletic children. Dr. Lynch is available for speaking engagements and consultations. His website is www.wayofchampions.com.

Chungliang Al Huang

Philosopher, performing artist, and internationally acclaimed Tao master, Chungliang Al Huang is the founder-president of the Living Tao Foundation and the international Lan Ting Institute in the sacred mountains in China, and on the Oregon Coast, USA. He is one of the most sought-after speakers in the fields of human potentiality, cultural diversity and creative dynamism in global business, education, and all arenas of life. He is a research scholar of the Academia Sinica, a Fellow of the World Academy of Art and Science, and an assembly member for the Council for a Parliament of the World Religions. He received the highest-rated speaker award from Young Presidents' Organization, the New Dimension

Broadcaster Award, and the prestigious Gold Medal from the Ministry of Education of the Republic of China. A close colleague and collaborator with the late scholar Alan Watts and mythologist Joseph Campbell, Huang was featured in the inaugural segment of Bill Moyers' renowned PBS *World of Ideas* series. He is the author of numerous best-selling books, including the classic *Embrace Tiger, Return to Mountain* and *Quantum Soup*; and co-author with Alan Watts of *Tao: The Watercourse Way* and with Dr. Jerry Lynch, *Thinking Body, Dancing Mind*; *Tao Mentoring, Working Out, Working Within*; and *The Way of the Champion*. His website is: www.livingtao.org.